A survey of the works of:

Keith Laumer

D.G. Compton

Robert Sheckley

Robert Moore Williams

Alan E. Nourse

H. Beam Piper

Managansett Press

Don D'Ammassa is the author of:

Horror
Blood Beast
Servant of Chaos*
Caverns of Chaos*
Wings over Manhattan
The Gargoyle
That Way Madness Lies*
Little Evils*
Passing Death*
Date with the Dark*
The Devil Is in the Details*
Living Things*
Shadows Over R'Lyeh*

Science Fiction
Scarab*
Haven*
Narcissus*
Translation Station
The Sinking Island*
Alien & Otherwise*
Wormdance*
Sandcastles*
Carbon Copies*
Phantom of the Space Opera*

Mysteries
Murder in Silverplate*
Dead of Winter*
Death at the Art Gallery*
Death on the Mountain*
Death on Black Island*
Death in Black and White*

Fantasy
The Kaleidoscope*
Elaborate Lies*
The Maltese Gargoyle*
Perilous Pursuits*
Multiplicity*
The Hippogriff of the Baskervilles*

Nonfiction
The Encyclopedia of Science Fiction
The Encyclopedia of Fantasy & Horror
The Encyclopedia of Adventure Fiction
Masters of Detection Vol I*
Masters of Detection Vol II*
Masters of Detection Vol III*
Masters of Horror Vol I*
Architects of Tomorrow Vol I*

*published by Managansett Press

ARCHITECTS OF TOMORROW
Volume I

Don D'Ammassa

Some of these essays were previously published in shorter form on the internet.

Copyright ©2015 by Don D'Ammassa. All rights reserved. If you would like to use material from this book other than brief excerpts for review purposes, prior written permission must be received by contacting the author at dondammassa@cox.net.

Managansett Press First Edition 2015

ARCHITECTS OF TOMORROW

CONTENTS

Introduction	7
Keith Laumer	9
D.G. Compton	44
Robert Sheckley	79
Robert Moore Williams	99
Alan E. Nourse	129
H. Beam Piper	147
Index of Titles	161

INTRODUCTION

    Science Fiction was long considered beneath the consideration of academics and not even serious book reviewers could be bothered with escape literature. The occasional fantastic novel by an establishment writer – *Nineteen Eighty-Four, Brave New World, The Handmaid's Tale, Slaughterhouse Five* – were all fiercely defended as not being science fiction at all. That has changed in recent years and there is a long row of books containing serious critical essays about science fiction and fantasy in my library. But has it changed all that much?

    There are actually only a handful of authors whose works have attracted serious and consistent attention. Philip K. Dick, Ursula K. Le Guin, and Ray Bradbury are the most frequent subjects of this attention. There are also occasional nods to a handful of writers whose popularity demands recognition – Robert A. Heinlein, J.R.R. Tolkien, J.K. Rowling, Neil Gaiman – but sometimes these seem almost grudging acknowledgments.

    Many of the writers who wrote prolifically and who were popular within the genre during their careers are never going to attract this kind of attention. They produced workmanlike fiction that satisfied their readers but they were not writing the kind of stories that lend themselves to detailed analysis. On the other hand, they really don't deserve to be buried in the anonymity of used book stores and specialty collections.

    The essays that make up this book are meant to survey their work and summarize it for those who might well never read any of the work being discussed. My hope, however, is that it will stir a few people at least to chase down those works which appeal to them so that the memories of these writers does not completely fade away.

    A note about gender. In these hypersensitive times, it might be noticed with displeasure that all of the authors covered here are male. This is partly a matter beyond my control. Although there are a significant number of women writing in the genre, most of the best of these are still working so a retrospective essay about their work is clearly premature.

That doesn't mean that there were no important female writers in the past. Catherine Moore, Andre Norton, James Tiptree/Alice Sheldon, Zenna Henderson, and several others come to mind. Leigh Brackett is one of my all time favorites and I seriously considered including her in this volume, but decided not to until I manage to track down one wayward novel not available to me.

But I haven't forgotten them and you shouldn't either.

KEITH LAUMER

Keith Laumer was a prolific writer whose output dropped dramatically following a stroke in 1971. He is probably best remembered for his Retief and Bolo stories, which is a shame because they are generally among his lesser work. Laumer was one of those writers who had a reputation for producing fast paced but unambitiou adventure stories and he was often overlooked for his considerable though uneven literary talents. He was in fact nominated for both the Hugo and Nebula awards on more than one occasion, although he never won. He had previously worked in the diplomatic service, which inspired his one mainstream novel and most of the Retief series, but his first published book was *Worlds of the Imperium* (1962), half of an Ace double.

Worlds of the Imperium introduced Brion Bayard, who would return for further adventures. He is mysteriously kidnapped at the beginning of the novel by agents of an alternate universe who are exploring our reality, which is among the few that were not destroyed by the development of a radical new technology. Bayard, who accepts his situation with aplomb, finds himself in a world where England, Germany, and Sweden have united as the Imperium with exclusive control of the technology to travel among alternate realities.

The Imperium, which does not have atomic weapons, is being attacked by another reality ruled by a ruthless dictator, who turns out to be that universe's version of Brion Bayard. The Imperium wants him to take the dictator's place so they can manipulate his culture but Bayard isn't sure that he wants the job. He narrowly escapes an attack by the enemy forces and then is forced to fight a duel with a local official whom he has publicly insulted. The mission gets off to a shaky start because no one realized that the two Bayards no longer look alike - the dictator lost his legs somewhere along the way - and the impersonation fails immediately. This seems like a rather fundamental failure of the Imperium's intelligence service.

Through a chain of contrived coincidences, Bayard falls in with the opposition to the tyrannical version of himself. His new allies only last an hour or two, however, before they are dispersed or killed by the repressive government's security forces. Our Bayard in and out of trouble several times after that before he finally meets his duplicate. At that meeting Bayard discovers that he has been lied to, and shortly afterward one of the Imperium officers shows up with a gang of thugs, kills the dictator, and captures our hero as part of a plot by a cabal within the Imperium to seize control of another Earth and use it as a powerbase to pressure their own government. It is not a great novel and there are too many coincidences – a flaw that will show up constantly in Laumer's work - but in general it was a solid and exciting adventure story mildly reminiscent of *The Thirty-Nine Steps* by John Buchan. It was certainly one of the more interesting Ace double novels.

A Trace of Memory – a full length novel - was serialized in 1962 and appeared in book form the next year. Legion is a drifter who has no self confidence and no prospects. He avoids arrest as a vagrant by pretending to have answered an advertisement by a man named Foster, even though he has no interest in a career as a soldier of fortune. Foster then tells him a strange story. He is suffering from amnesia but believes that he is at least a century old. He has a notebook made of material unknown to scientists on Earth and claims that he is being pursued by an enemy that manifests itself as arrays of strange lights in the darkness.

The reader will be well ahead of Legion thanks to a prologue which shows an alien space traveler stranded on Earth in the remote past, along with a glimpse of the mysterious Hunters. Legion plans to slip away at the first opportunity but coincidentally - to speed up the plot - the Hunters show up again before he can do so. Another coincidence has Foster regenerating to a younger version of himself that same night. Before long the police are after Legion because they believe he murdered the older version, even though they have no body.

Young Foster also has a new case of amnesia. The two of them both become fugitives from the law, as well as the Hunters. They decipher part of the notebook and decide that the lair of the monsters is at Stonehenge in England. Foster wants to investigate immediately but Legion just wants to clear his name and forget about everything that has happened.

At Stonehenge, they survive another attack and activate a device that calls a lifeboat from a large orbiting spaceship. They board the lifeboat and conveniently find training tapes that enable them to use the equipment and eventually restore part of Foster's memory, enough that he knows that he has been stranded on Earth for centuries - it turns out he was King Arthur. Humans, it appears, are descended from castaways of his race - although Laumer never explains what happened to the hominids in the fossil record.

    Foster has no idea why he was in the solar system, why he is being hunted, or what disaster led to the deaths of everyone else aboard the mother ship. He also explains that Terran humans would be able to regenerate like himself if they were vaccinated against getting old, a rather glib explanation of his longevity. The Hunters are eventually revealed to be a form of lie that can only be nourished by electrical energy, which confines them for the most part to the area of the hidden underground installation under Stonehenge. One has to wonder how they could have evolved under those circumstances since electricity is not normally abundant in the natural world but Laumer never explains.

    Foster takes his ship and returns to his home world, but Legion takes the lifeboat full of technological wonders and returns to Earth where he quietly amasses a small fortune and builds a retreat in an island off the coast of Peru. There, inexplicably, he puts all his artifacts in one spot with limited security and fail to even work out an escape plan to use when, inevitably, someone comes in force to find out where he is getting all these technological marvels. Laumer resorts to coincidence constantly to keep the story moving. Both Soviet and American strike forces arrive within hours of one another, resulting in a pitched battle during which Legion escapes, eventually makes his way to the hidden lifeboat, and then goes off to find his former mentor among the stars.

    Arriving on the alien home world, he discovers that their civilization has collapsed into a form of primitive slave holding and that no one remembers their previously exalted past. He wanders around with a cat, who coincidentally and implausibly shows up at the precise moment necessary to enable him to escape a prison. Since authority in this society is based on personal combat, he decides to challenge the local ruler and eventually overthrows the entire planetary government. The first half of the novel carries the reader along with its breathless action and the series of mysteries revealed, but the entire second half of the novel rings false, artificial and overly contrived.

ARCHITECTS OF TOMORROW

Envoy to New Worlds (1963) was the first collection of Retief stories. Jame Retief is a minor diplomat in the Terrestrial diplomatic service, and he bears a strong resemblance to the Brion Bayard character in *Embassy* which is discussed below. The Retief stories are almost invariably written to a formula. His superiors are exaggerated buffoons, most frequently represented by a halfwit named Magnan, but he usually makes them look good by disobeying their orders and solving the problems between humans and one or another alien species.

Humans in general always come off looking bad, but usually the aliens fare no better. In "Protocol" (aka "The Yillian Way") the aliens treat the human mission with extreme disrespect until Retief rebels and meets them on their own terms. The Yill are portrayed as honorable, if somewhat strange, and prone to intolerance. That's not the case in "Sealed Orders" (aka "Retief of Red Tape Mountain". This time Retief is supposed to intercede in a battle between human settlers and manta like aliens both of whom claim a rather desolate planet. He discovers (or actually intuits) that this is all a game for the aliens, tricks the leader of the local group into engaging in personal combat, defeats him, and then negotiates a division of the planet favorable to both sides. The aliens in this case are childish and easily fooled, though the humans are equally incompetent.

"Cultural Exchange" is a bit contrived, and none of the various parties are alien this time. There is a complicated plot involving the shipment of a large number of supposed students and various armaments which are actually intended to be an invasion force. Retief manipulates everyone concerned to thwart the invasion, saves an imperiled wine crop, and favorably alter the balance of power in a cluster of human settled worlds, much to the chagrin of his superiors.

"Aide Memoire" introduces rivalry with the Groaci, an alien race less prone to putting incompetents in positions of authority, although they always proved less resourceful than Retief. "Policy" is not very good. Retief is on the Groaci homeworld and manages to discover the fate of a missing Terran starship simply by accosting a local drunk and then browbeating a government representative into admitting everything. The humans are even more inept than usual and Retief unaccountably doesn't transmit his information until it is too late for it to have any effect. "Palace Revolution" (aka "Gambler's World") is also fairly weak. Discovering a planned coup on a primitive world, Retief engages in some not very convincing negotiations with a casino owner who is behind the rebellion and saves the day.

A Plague of Demons (1965 - a shorter version was serialized as *The Hounds of Hell*) is one of Laumer's many novels dealing with a superhuman. John Bravais is called to Algeria by an old friend who has been forced to go undercover. He learns two disturbing things almost immediately. First, the US government - and possibly several foreign powers - are developing surgical techniques to create super soldiers. Second, people are disappearing around the world in unprecedented numbers.

When Bravais stumbles upon an alien creature dissecting a human, he tries to report it to the local United Nations command, only to discover that the commander and some of his men are superpowered allies of the alien, which forces him to become a fugitive. He subsequently learns that in addition to their enhanced human allies, the aliens have mental powers which can make them appear as normal humans for short periods of time. His partner succumbs to their influence and Bravais finds himself on his own, although he now has acquired some enhancements of his own. The first half of the novel is in fact one extended chase sequence, with our hero escaping Algeria aboard a disreputable cargo ship, evading capture repeatedly when he returns to the United States and then sets out to visit a location his dead partner suggested as a safe haven. Laumer is at his best here, with a crisp and reasonably plausible narrative enlivened by intelligent and sometimes clever prose.

The second half of the novel lets down a bit, although it does introduce the concept of the Bolos, human brains installed in supertanks, which would reappear in Laumer's later fiction and spawn a series of stories and novels by other authors. Bravais is eventually captured and awakens to find himself ensconced in a fighting machine on a distant planet, where he is able to regain his self identity and probe the minds of his alien captors, turning the situation to his advantage. How he acquires these mental powers is never really explained.

The aliens are also meant to represent Good and Evil in some mystical fashion. The closing chapters are overly ambitious. Not only does our hero penetrate to the center of an alien stronghold, lead a successful revolt against the mind controllers, and personally wrestle another alien life form to death, but he also organizes an army to resist a renewed conquest and alerts the Earth to the danger, providing a plan to expunge the invisible aliens living secretly among humans. He finishes up by launching an interstellar war against the aliens. Laumer did have a tendency to rush his endings, and this is a notable example.

The Great Time Machine Hoax (1964, aka *A Hoax in Time*) is a broad farce that makes little effort to be plausible. The protagonist is due to inherit an expense ridden estate from an uncle when he discovers that a self aware computer was built beneath the mansion and provided with unlimited data. The computer has expanded on its original mission and now contains so much information that it can reconstruct actual historical events with incredible (and totally implausible) detail.

The first effort to explore this function goes awry when the protagonist, a friend, and an avatar of the computer become lost in a succession of past and future realities - Laumer never explains how all of this including enormous distances could be created within the context of a small chamber, or how they could possibly live that long without access to food and other supplies from the "real" world, but none of that is particularly relevant to the story. Laumer frequently resorted to absurdity in his fiction, particularly in the Retief stories, but there is rarely any genuinely inventive humor. He often repeats the same joke endlessly, as though absurdity was in itself funny, and it doesn't work in this novel at all.

Eventually the reader is told that the characters really have been projected through time - just how that is possible given the setup is not explained either - and their presence has altered history beyond recognition. Despite this, neither of the story's two titles makes any sense, since there is no hoax involved. We do see the first glimmer of Laumer's political philosophy stated clearly when our hero falls in with a bunch of lazy anarchists. "Most of the shrill cries of social injustice come from people who contribute nothing to the scene..." This sentiment will crop up more often in his later work.

Embassy (1965) is not science fiction, although its protagonist is Brion Bayard, the same name used in *Worlds of the Imperium*. Bayard is an unorthodox - i.e. honest and competent - junior diplomat assigned to the corrupt American embassy in the mythical nation of Samoy. Laumer also employs the odd convention of having

Bayard's viewpoint scenes told in first person while the bulk of the book is in third person.

There is an interesting double standard in this book. One of his criticisms of the senior diplomats is that they are all racists who think of the locals as stereotypes, relatively stupid, lazy, and lacking in courage or principle. But then Laumer portrays each and every one of the local characters in just those terms, everything from a simple minded communist agitator to an absurdly unrealistic would be dictator to a pair of lazy file clerks. The diplomats themselves are engaged in chicanery and open corruption. They are more interested in lining their pockets than advancing the interests of either the American government or the Samoyan people.

The main plot involves a plan to sneak high powered arms into the country to suppress a communist rebellion and then seize control of the government, except that no one actually has control of the weapons which in any case end up making little difference. There is also a completely unbelievable sequence in which a rather dumb American businessman comes to Samoy with no plan or contacts, simply to find out if there are any investment opportunities, and he relies on the word of the first random American visitor he meets. Laumer clearly had no future as a writer of plausible political thrillers.

Galactic Diplomat (1966) is the second collection of Retief stories, and there are hints that Laumer might have temporarily exhausted his store of ideas for this format because the selection is sometimes repetitive, sometimes incongruous. The opening story, "Ultimatum", is for example another one in which aliens threaten an attack until Retief calls their bluff and co-opts them into working for the humans instead of against them. "Saline Solution", however, inexplicably has Retief and Magnan working in the asteroid belt with no hint of aliens or even interstellar travel. They are caught in the middle of an attempt by a big mining corporation to jump the claim of an independent and Retief resorts to the company's own tyle of trickery to outwit them. "The Brass God" (aka "Retief: God Speaker") doesn't even attempt to be a serious story. Retief and company deal with an alien religion whose adherents are comic book style caricatures.

"The Castle of Light" is slightly better. The Groaci, Retief's recurring foe, attempt to occupy a neutral planet by taking advantage of peculiarities of interstellar war and an unusual festival that occurs only once in several generations. Retief fails to save the day this time. It turns out the festival coincides with an astronomical event that causes devastating earthquakes and the Groaci are wiped out without his intervention. "Wicker Wonderland" is another slight change of pace. Retief is working for a Groaci diplomat, who is both competent and virtuous, when he uncovers a plot by humans against the local native population. The story jumps around and the pace is so even that it feels like several sketches were patched together and it is never clear how Retief ended up working for the Groaci.

"Native Intelligence" (aka "The Governor of Glave") is a thinly disguised diatribe against what Laumer apparently perceives as freeloading by ignorant but rapacious people who use "popular" revolutions to enhance their status because they are neither ambitious nor smart enough to work for a living. In this instance they are engaged in taking over a previously prosperous planet until Retief singlehandedly restores the old order. "There's always a certain percentage of any population with a conviction that society is a conspiracy to deny them their rights. The right to be totally ignorant of any useful knowledge seems to be the basic one."

The next story is "The Prince and the Pirate", better written but still a polemic about governments who impose the needs of the majority on the more successful - hence entitled - minority. It is not surprising that writers with this world view opposing what they see as the evils of welfare are generally favorably disposed toward monarchies. "Courier" is quite good. Retief is sent to help a human colony fend off an invasion by nasty aliens, abetted by crooked humans. The final story, "Protest Note", is the least interesting. Retief forces a treaty on interlopers by beating up their chief.

Retief's War (1971, expanded from the 1965 version) was Retief's first novel length adventure, set on a planet whose variegated inhabitants are essentially part machine, most of them moving on wheels. A crooked Terran diplomat, an ambitious and nasty local tribal leader, and a wily Groaci spy conspire to overthrow the semi-anarchy that has long prevailed, each for reasons of his own. Retief finds himself leading a rebellion by uniting several of the tribes in what could have been a fairly serious adventure but devolves into farce. Retief actually disguises himself as an alien for much of the book. There are a few semi-relevant subplots and lots of running around but this is basically a very long version of the standard Retief adventure among dumb aliens.

The Other Side of Time (1965) is the sequel to *Worlds of the Imperium*. Bayard discovers that there are other timelines that think they control the multiverse when he stumbles upon an invading force of hulking hominids and is taken prisoner. There is also a third race from another hominid strain, and they also consider themselves the true masters of the universe. Neither of these are actually human. He escapes from the first group only to be captured by the second. No one he encounters from either civilization is particularly honorable, human or otherwise.

Laumer refers to one of the alien species as cannibals, which is nonsense since they don't eat their own kind. They do eat humans, however. The plot is structured like many of Laumer's novels - a succession of captures and escapes and other minor crises - then when he reaches the desired word count, he brings it to a sudden end, not always completely successfully, as is evident here. Bayard gets stranded in a low tech world but through an astounding series of coincidences is able to build an inter-reality transport device almost from scratch, and then finds his way back to another viable timeline through another series of coincidences. It is more than slightly frustrating that the plot is so contrived because Laumer's prose is quite good. The climax comes out of nowhere with Bayard rescued again, and this time he invents a time machine on the spot so that he can go back to before the Imperium timeline was destroyed and prevent the disaster from happening. Happy ending but not a very well crafted one.

Earthblood (1966) was written in collaboration with Rosel George Brown and appears to be set in the Retief universe, long after the Terran empire has fallen. There are references to bolos and the Groaci. The protagonist is a rare purebred human in a galaxy where humans have interbred with some alien races or mutant strains, producing Geeks, and interact with several separate alien species called Gooks. That alone conveys a great deal about the racial attitudes of the novel, but it is more complicated than that. Reflecting the dichotomy prevalent in the Retief stories, we have several incidents where tolerance of the different and friendship with aliens is commended, but at the same time the reader is told that the human race was the only species to experience altruism, to build memorable cities, and so forth and so on. This is particularly unsatisfying because when our hero finally is reunited with a pure human civilization, he finds them to be just as stupid and self serving as were the various aliens he encountered.

Roan's adventures along the way are individually much more interesting. He is raised by an alien and a halfbreed, is kidnapped into an interstellar circus and captured by space pirates, becomes leader of the pirates, then defeats a robot warship left over from a possibly extinct alien race, locates the remnants of the human empire, gets involved in a civil war, is appointed grand admiral, and lives unhappily ever after..

Lafayette O'Leary made his debut in *The Time Bender* (1966, aka *Axe and Dragon*), which skirts the border between science fiction and fantasy. O'Leary is a nerdish type who experiments with self hypnosis and dream states and finds himself in an alternate world, Artesia, which is a forerunner of modern steampunk fiction with steam powered vehicles and other anachronisms in a medieval setting.

O'Leary can alter this reality through force of will at times, but not always, as suits the purposes of the author. The story is lightly humorous throughout, and for the first third our hero still believes it is all just a dream, even when he is arrested for practicing sorcery. There is actually no magic in it although the explanations of how things are actually accomplished are pretty flimsy. Our hero saves the kingdom from its usurper, who is also from another reality, defeats a dragon which is actually a displaced dinosaur, kills the leader of the barbarian horde, outwits the schemers, and rescues the princess, only to discover he is the long lost ruler of Artesia, which honor he declines when he realizes that both he and the princess love someone else. Laumer left things open for a sequel by noting that the organization which polices the alternate realities - not the same one as in the Bayard stories - have noted that he might make a good agent for them in the future. Lightweight and episodic, but more integrated than the earlier Laumer novels and quite amusing most of the time.

Laumer's next two novels were stand alone and neither were very good. *The Monitors* (1966) was made into a low budget and very bad movie. The monitors are alien invaders who are indistinguishable from humans and all speak flawless English. They take over the planet all at once, replacing all governments, police, and other authority figures and imposing a rigidly determined interpretation of our laws - some of which are admittedly absurd - for the good of the human race. They cannot understand why there is resistance, but of course there is.

The novel is openly satirical but many of the arguments made by the aliens to criticize human foibles are clearly contrived to be one sided, which blunts the sarcasm. The story is revealed through the eyes of one stubborn man who discovers that most humans, including the resistance movement, are just as dumb as the invaders. This is a moderately good short story idea spun out to novel length, and some of the incidents are clearly just filler to push up the word count. The jokes are rarely funny and they are repeated so often that they lose every trace of humor by the end of the book.

Catastrophe Planet (1966 - later reissued as *The Breaking Earth* with a couple of short stories added) was not much better. The earth's crust has broken loose and there are devastating earthquakes, tornadoes, and volcanoes all over the world. Mal Irish is a not entirely reputable drifter who finds a dying man in the wreckage of a building. The man that he was part of an expedition to Antarctica which had intended to create a compensating force - not a very plausible scenario - but which was wiped out mysteriously after finding evidence of an ancient technological civilization. The dying man was being pursued by mysterious strangers - three of whom Irish kills in short order - but as a result it is now our hero that they are looking for.

The coincidences this time are almost comically contrived. Irish takes a coin from the dead man and somehow not only do the bad guys know that he has it, they also have an entire contingent of supposed numismatists staying at the hotel where he takes refuge in Miami, and naturally he takes the coin to one of them for identification. The man switch coins on him, for no good reason, but Irish realizes this and decides to find out why. He follows the conspirators secretly that night and rescues a young woman they are trying to abduct, a woman who speaks no known language.

Another coincidence saves his life when an earthquake throws off the aim of a man about to shoot him at close range. The woman is captured again and based on virtually no evidence, he decides to look for her on the island of Crete, which isn't an island any more.

Once there he almost immediately meets someone who has been ferrying mysterious parties out to an empty spot of the sea where they dive and disappear. He decides to investigate by diving down at that spot, and he finds an undersea city.

When he enters the city, he immediately runs into a lone guard who conveniently speaks English. Then he captures another, who even more conveniently has the missing girl's clothing in his possession. Irish also just happened to bring a cutting torch with him, which he uses to escape from a locked tunnel. He then steals a boat, which just happens to contain a military style machinegun hidden inside, but not hidden well enough. The mystery men also conveniently speak English when Irish is spying on them.

The steady string of unbelievable coincidences is symptomatic of lazy plotting and it is likely Laumer wrote this one very quickly and without devoting much thought to the plot. In the final thirty pages we discover that the girl is the last survivor of a prehistoric race, preserved by suspended animation, and that the mystery men are actually a race of nonhuman creatures from somewhere else who prey on humans. The hero destroys them all and rescues the girl. All of this takes place so quickly that it feels more like an outline than a climax.

Planet Run (1966) was Laumer's second and final novel collaboration, this one with Gordon R. Dickson. It was very minor work for either writer. A long-retired space explorer is lured into one last mission to stake a claim on a distant planet, accompanied by a comically naive young man. They survive several encounters with bad guys and raw nature, find a gateway to another part of the galaxy, and thwart the chief villain who has been working behind the scenes. The story is occasionally ludicrous and badly plotted. At one point we are told that humanity doesn't have a faster than light drive but we never hear how then it is possible to travel from one star to another so quickly. The supposedly experienced character makes so many rudimentary mistakes and bad judgments that there is no real contrast between him and the greenhorn.

The Invaders (1967, aka *Meteor Men*) was the first of two books Laumer wrote tied to the frequently inept television series, so some of the dumb things in the story were probably not his fault. David Vincent is a manufacturing consultant - except that no consultant makes extraordinary recommendations based on a one hour tour of a plant - who coincidentally has noticed four strange components at four different plants which can be assembled into something that looks like a ray gun. The final component was made at still another plant where he is also called in to consult, but the local security officer insists that information about the unit is classified - which is nonsense since it wasn't a government contract, there was no confidentiality agreement involved, and in any case he could not overrule his superior.

The security man is an alien, whose skin is painfully hot to touch, yet no one has ever noticed this before! Vincent steals the drawings of the last component and with a scientist friend builds one to complete the weapon in his possession. It projects a cone of "negative space", whatever that might mean. They call the FBI who immediately agree to send a team to investigate, which is patently absurd. Vincent never told them exactly what he learned and he has no particular standing with law enforcement. Nor is it clear how the aliens discover his involvement.

Vincent is captured and his friend is injured and develops amnesia. The aliens incidentally communicate to their mother ship in English, conveniently allowing Vincent to learn more about them by eavesdropping. Following the first section which is essentially the pilot episode, there are two further adventures, one involving Vincent's encounter with a madman who believes in the invaders but thinks Vincent is one of them. This is an extraordinarily bad story. The third and last isn't much better. Vincent hears that a meteor cloud – whatever that is - is likely to hit the Earth's atmosphere. He talks to a prominent scientist for five minutes and convinces him that there is a potentially great danger that no one previously suspected.

Nine by Laumer (1967) is a collection of short stories accompanied by an essay in which Harlan Ellison rather effusively calls him the best new science fiction writer since Kurt Vonnegut. The opening story is "Hybrid", in which roving space travelers find a fallen tree that is actually an alien intelligence that transforms itself from animal to plant late in its life cycle. One of them becomes host to the tree's offspring/spores in return for extended life and an improved physiology.

"End As a Hero" (later expanded into a novel) is about the only human survivor of an encounter with the alien Gool, who use a form of mind control and who are at war with Earth. Neither Laumer nor the copy editor knew how to spell "pseudo" and the plot doesn't make much sense. Why would humans be working to create a working mental defense system when they don't know at the timeabout the aliens' abilities? Why would they send a spy if they already know that his mind might be suborned, then immediately plan to kill him before he can return, and decide to disregard anything he tells them?

Contact with the aliens allows the protagonist to develop super-psi powers of his own and he is able to take control of minds down on Earth and compel them to let him through the defensive shield. It never occurs to him to control the minds of the people in charge. The story doesn't work dramatically either because since he can make his way in and out of guarded facilities simply by manipulating a few minds, there is no real challenge.

"The Walls", on the other hand, is quite good. In a massively urbanized future, an obnoxious husband has full wall televisions installed in his apartment, which ultimately drives his wife insane. "Dinochrome" (aka "Combat Unit") is reminiscent of Colin Kapp's earlier "Gottlos." It's a Bolo story about a malfunctioning supertank that turns on its owners. "Placement Test" is a satire about a future where people are medically dumbed down so that they are content doing menial jobs. This one also starts off pretty well. It also has one of the classic SF failures of prophecy - the computers of the far future all use tape reels. But what starts as a criticism of bureaucracy ends up as advocacy of elitism. Our hero has been deliberately treated badly so that he can prove that he is one of the few qualified to run the world. We are even told that the idea that "the will of the people equals wisdom" is "folklore." The conclusion is that the only people worthwhile are those who are willing to cheat and lie to get what they want, and therefore the repressive system Laumer described is actually Utopian rather than Dystopian.

"Doorstep" is trivial. A Wellsian style space capsule lands on Earth and an overly zealous general kills its passenger before discovering that it is friendly. "The Long Remembered Thunder" is one of Laumer's better efforts. A scientist is sent to his home town to locate the source of peculiar transmissions which are interfering with a government project. He is particularly interested in a mysterious and very elderly recluse who is never seen during the hours of darkness, and who has told one confidant that he battles demons in his basement. Unfortunately, some local punks have wounded him and tried unsuccessfully to burn down his house, and he is nowhere to be found. The story falters toward the end, with a deus ex machina device for defeating the alien invaders and another to turn time backwards and let the elderly lovers correct their youthful mistake. Not bad overall though.

"Cocoon" is another story of television as a device to sedate the masses, and a rebel movement aimed at disrupting them. Last in the collection is "A Trip to the City" (aka "It Could Be Anything"). This is the best story in the collection. A young man who has never left the small town where he lives discovers that the outside world he knows through magazines and television does not exist, that he is actually in a wasteland surrounded by cities populated with automatons that have a limited range of actions mimicking humans. The reader never finds out what's going on but this is deliberate. The point of the story is that nothing is real unless we go see it ourselves.

The Day Before Forever and Thunderhead (1967) consists of a novella and a novelette. The protagonist of the first and longer story wakes up in the 22nd Century but remembers living in the 20th. He is soon on the run from the repressive police of a future in which a megacorporation that dispenses longevity rules the world. After various adventures he penetrates to the heart of the company and discovers it is run by an older version of himself, that he is the latest in a line of programmed clones originally designed to provide a succession of likeminded CEOs, although the system has been corrupted by the discovery of literal immortality. There are a few holes in the plot but they are small ones and the writing is some of the best Laumer ever did, although it also reflects his elitist views. The hero decides that a benevolent dictatorship is better for humanity than freedom. The second story is not as good. A forgotten military picket on a remote and neglected colony world continues to do his duty even though he has lost all contact with his superiors. He gives his life to help avoid an alien landing in a rather sappy, melodramatic fashion.

Enemies from Beyond (1967) was a second Invaders tie-in, and like the first it consists of three short adventures. Laumer made no real attempt to construct plausible explanations of any of the logical fallacies in the television show. In the first story, Vincent hears of the sinking of a commercial freighter and concludes - rightly - that aliens were responsible, so he rushes to the hospital, convinced that minutes count - toward what? - and the doctor in charge is easily convinced to break the rules and let him in because since he has no government identification he must therefore be a government agent.

Then, as it happens, Vincent knows not only of the existence of a radically new submarine despite its top secret status, he is also a personal friend of the captain! He convinces his friend not only to take him out on one of the secret missions, but to re-route it to the scene of the freighter sinking. Then he just happens to run into a salvage operator who has access to a state of the art torpedo. He bluffs another man into spilling confidential information in the second story, no more plausibly than in the first. This one involves sea creatures coming ashore and attacking people, which seem like a poor tactic for invaders who want to remain unsuspected. The final story involves Vincent's encounter with a clairvoyant who can read the aliens' minds, sort of, and reveals another string of incredible coincidences. This is, frankly, an embarrassingly bad book from cover to cover.

Galactic Odyssey (1967, serialized as *Spaceman*) is a showcase of Laumer's faults, unfortunately. Episodic, hastily written, filled with coincidences and implausibilities, it opens with the hero, Billy Danger, taking shelter in a grain silo that turns out to be an interstellar spaceship run by alien hunters who just happen to speak English all the time. At one of their hunting stops, everyone is killed except Billy and the inevitable beautiful maiden. They are stranded on that uninhabited world but just happen to stumble upon a seven thousand year old spaceship with a workable interstellar warning beacon. Unfortunately they attract the attention of non-human aliens who abduct the girl and leave Billy to die, although obviously he survives and eventually is rescued by another passing ship. There follows a series of adventures as he attempts to find and rescue the girl, during the course of which he is imprisoned, enslaved, employed as a spy, becomes captain of his own ship, and eventually completes the mission.

Retief and the Warlords (1968) is a novel and introduces the Haterakans as the primary alien villains, although the Groaci are back as well. The Terran authorities refuse to help the various human colonies and miners working in a newly opened region of space, preferring outreach programs to the lobsterlike Haterakans. As usual the plot is helped along by a liberal application of absurd coincidences and the tone is light and even silly at times. The diplomats are so stupid that any traces of verisimilitude are eradicated. Retief is captured briefly by the Haterakans, escapes improbably by seizing control of a ship, and arrives among the beleaguered colonists. They in turn make him a prisoner and he is forced to escape again, this time with the assistance of a stranded Haterakan. But then he finds himself a prisoner of the aliens again.

This all gets pretty monotonous by half way through the novel. Retief even makes use of some time stop capsules so he can extricate himself from a series of improbable circumstances. Retief then reorganizes the Keystone Cops style Terran Defense Legion and thwarts the aliens without causing significant casualties on either side Although all of this is mildly amusing, it is more of an extended joke than a serious novel.

Assignment in Nowhere (1968) is a Brion Bayard novel, although this time he is not the protagonist. He rescues Johnny Curlon from what appears to be our timeline but is then attacked by minions from another reality. Curlon is the last descendant of Richard the Lionhearted and he is the nexus of powerful forces which could save, or destroy, all of the alternate timelines. For some reason the blighted worlds where civilization died are expanding and the nearby timelines are seeing influxes of corrosion, rust, and toadstools. Picturesque, but not particularly logical.

Curlon is captured, escapes, is captured, escapes, is captured, and escapes in the same pattern as is prevalent in most of Laumer's novels, although like the previous Bayard adventures, this one is considerably better written. Briefly Curlon teams up with the sinister Baron Van Roosevelt who convinces him that he is trying to restore balance to the universe, although eventually it is revealed that he is actually attempting to restructure time for his own purposes. The rules about changing realities are pretty fluid; Laumer obviously didn't spend a lot of time thinking them through. This one feels more like fantasy than science fiction despite the attempts to provide rational explanations.

It's a Mad, Mad, Mad Galaxy (1968) provides further evidence that Laumer was better at shorter length, starting with the opening story, " The Body Builders", a lively satire in which people live in tanks with their consciousness transmitted to a variety of robotic bodies. Laumer characterizes this as a logical extension of makeup and more invasive methods of improving one's appearance. The protagonist is inadvertently dumped into his actual body and eventually discovers that he likes it better. "The Planet Wreckers" on the other hand is not so good. The hero discovers that Earth is the set for an alien produced disaster movie with real disasters. Occasionally funny, more often just silly.

"The Star-Sent Knaves" (aka "The Time Thieves") is more or less a sequel, this time with alien art thieves using superscience to perform their heists. "The War With the Yukks" is about the accidental discovery of an ancient automated weapons system in Honduras. This one might have been a much better story if it had been handled straightforwardly, but Laumer plays this one for minor laughs as well and whatever tension might have existed in the plot is wasted. The last story is in the same vein. "Goobereality" is about an invention that extrapolates realities, but the inventor learns that someone has stolen the plans for his device. Not bad but minor.

Greylorn (1968) starts off with the title story, one of Laumer's less satisfying novelettes. Earth is about to be overwhelmed by some unexplained form of pink tide so the authorities send a slower than light starship to a colony they hope was successfully founded fifty years earlier, hoping that the colonists will be able to help. The captain puts down multiple mutinies during the five year flight, then outsmarts a ship full of aliens in a completely implausible fashion, finds the colony, which just happens to have developed better ships and newer weapons which can destroy the pink tide. It doesn't seem likely that a newly planted colony could have progressed that far in just over a generation.

"The Night of the Trolls" is much better. A man wakens from a sensory deprivation experiment that somehow induced suspended animation to discover that forty years have passed and that a devastating war has reduced the outside world to feudalism. (He gets a hint of this when a seventy year old book crumples to dust.) He meets the local baron, also a recent escapee from suspended animation, and foils his plans of world conquest. The surprise - an old man who helps him turns out to be his son - is unfortunately very obvious from the outset. This was a pretty good story but the conclusion - he helps launch a starship - seems incongruous given the situation on Earth.

ARCHITECTS OF TOMORROW

"The Other Sky" is about the secret conquest of Earth by the alien Niss, whom the government refers to as guests. The set up is not entirely plausible and the typical Laumer dependence upon coincidence is in evidence. The hero just happens to have a secret exit from his apartment that he discovered by accident. He finds another alien, a friendly one from some kind of alternate world on Pluto - which has just been knocked out of its orbit - and also finds out that he used to be part of the space navy, which he doesn't remember at all. This was a kind of kitchen sink plot that introduces new factors so rapidly that it's hard to immediately notice the inconsistencies, and has much of the feel of the Rull stories by A.E. van Vogt. The final third, set on the alternate Pluto, is so implausible that the exotic strangeness evoked early on dissipates completely. "The King of the City" isn't bad but it's pretty minor. A space squadron comes back to find that Earth, or at least the US, has fallen into anarchy, and after various secretive movements they depose the shadow government and restore order.

Laumer wrote three quite short novels tied to the British television program *The Avengers* in 1968. They are *The Afrit Affair, The Drowned Queen*, and *The Gold Bomb*. The first one has Emma Peel as Steed's partner; the other two feature Tara King. Steed is detailed to protect a group of diplomats at a special conference which has been threatened by someone calling himself the Afrit. Emma Peel is conspicuous by her absence, but female characters were quite noticeably rare in Laumer's previous fiction, and none of them were portrayed as being particularly competent or self reliant. Eventually she does show up, after a plague of pranks and odd events hounds the conference. Laumer captures some of the feeling of the show, but does not successfully negotiate the balance between humor and adventure that was essential to the program's success. Instead he has produced what is essentially a parody of the television program, and not a very funny one either.

The Drowned Queen is closer to science fiction. Steed and Tara King are working undercover aboard the world's first submersible luxury liner - which doesn't seem like a viable business model. There is a murder followed by other strange goings on and while the jokes aren't quite as overwhelming as in the first, there is still enough silliness to spoil the plot. The chief villain wants to hijack the ship and turn it into a pirate vessel, which would be a very impractical endeavor given its size and ease of detection. *The Gold Bomb* is no better. Steed and King have to track down a maniac who is building an atomic bomb for use in the British Isles. They succeed after a lackluster series of minor adventures.

Retief: Ambassador to Space (1969) is the third collection of Retief's shorter adventures. The formula had worn pretty thin by this point. "Giant Killer" involves killing a dinosaurlike creature to establish diplomatic credentials and "The Forbidden City" (aka "Retief, War Criminal") has him involved with the usual hijinx on a decadent planet. Retief saves the day against all odds. "Grime and Punishment" (aka "Clear As Mud") has some smart aliens for a change, and even the dumb humans aren't entirely hopeless. They have to deal with a crisis on a planet menaced by mud volcanoes and in the process secure a lucrative trade agreement. In "Dam Nuisance" – which is a parody of North Korea - Retief has to rescue Magnan, his superior, who is taken prisoner by aliens. He uses clever subterfuges to thwart an alliance by a neutral world with a hostile power in "Trick or Treaty", which is probably the single best Retief story. A Groaci plot to steal a planet from a race of intelligent balloons is foiled in "The Forest in the Sky" and a warlike, but not too bright, species must be shown the light in "Truce or Consequences." With the one exception mentioned, these are all very minor stories.

The Long Twilight (1969, aka *And Now They Wake*) predates the movie *Highlander*, which Laumer might well have sued for stealing his idea. In the near future, a form of broadcast power is inaugurated which triggers the awareness of two immortals, one of whom is in prison for having killed a man, the other of whom has become an alcoholic drifter. At the same time a peculiar, stationary tornado appears over the ocean. Through flashbacks we learn that the two of them are actually the source of the legend of the rivalry between Thor and Loki, based on a misunderstanding in the distant past. Both are actually aliens stranded on Earth and, as we eventually learn, both are reasonably nice guys.

The power station's artificial intelligence refuses to allow itself to be shut down and all the humans stationed there are killed by excessive heat and some kind of force field, while the tornado spawns a storm that threatens the eastern half of North America. The misunderstanding between the two immortals was contrived by a sentient warship that considers itself their master rather than their servant, and it is only when they destroy the ship - and thereby somehow lose their immortality - that they can be free and the Earth saved. Atypically for a Laumer novel, the chief protagonist dies on the last page. This was far and away Laumer's best novel at this point in his career, mixing his imaginative skills with a reasonably plausible plot.

The House in November (1970, aka *Seeds of Gonyl*) is also quite good until the halfway mark, despite some familiar faults. It is likely that Laumer began to care more about the quality of his writing during this period. Jeff Mallory wakes up one day to discover that three months of his life are missing. His town is completely enclosed by a metal wall, there is an enormous tower just beyond the town limits, and one of his daughters is missing. His wife and children don't remember the missing girl, and the door to her room has been plastered over. He also finds dead people scattered through the town, lying where they fell, and the rest of the population is clearly brainwashed, working every day in an installation on some project they don't understand and cannot describe. Creatures that look vaguely but not convincingly human can also be seen overseeing things but the protagonist avoids a close encounter.

Obviously it's some kind of alien invasion involving mind control. For some reason the protagonist's conditioning has worn off. He escapes the town and discovers that the people in the surrounding area believe the country has been conquered by the Russians. They discount his story of aliens as a paranoid fantasy. When he finally finds the army, a Russian-American alliance, they are similarly deluded, believing that the Chinese have invaded. Each population he encounters is subject to a different form of brainwashing, but for what overall purpose?

Continuing the episodic nature of the story, Mallory next encounters a group that believes that Satan and imps are responsible. There are several small coincidences that help him along, but they're not as outrageous as in some of the earlier novels. Then everything falls apart in the second half. We are told that the entire population of the world was wiped out by the invading aliens - who are a mass mind virus - except the people in the town where Mallory lived. This contradicts the existence of the other groups he encountered, which Laumer never explains. We are also expected to believe that except for the people in the town, everyone actually believes the nonsense they have been spouting despite clear evidence to the contrary.

Mallory discovers that he is descended from one of two alien guardians planted on Earth to watch for just such an invasion. Coincidentally he happened to be in the only town spared. Laumer never explains why his subconscious trigger did not throw off the conditioning until it was almost too late to stop the aliens. Fortunately, the secret base established by the good aliens is within walking distance of the town - another astounding coincidence - and after disposing of the second guardian - who has gone bad - Mallory discovers that he has super mental powers, can control humans, and can prevent the aliens from sporing. If the good aliens could do this, why is their initial decision to sterilize the planet? Why would the communications equipment require that both guardians cooperate to use it when its purpose was to report a crisis - like the death of one of the guardians? The ending is rushed and the details of the plot do not bear close examination.

Lafayette O'Leary returns in *The World Shuffler* (1970). For someone who has learned to travel between realities, he is awfully slow on the uptake when the palace where he lives suddenly becomes deserted and slightly rearranged, and he finds that everyone he knows has forgotten him and has led a different life. Accompanied by the woman he thinks of as a princess - though she's now a barmaid - he sets off on a series of the usual anecdotal and rather silly adventures. He is taken prisoner by shifty sailors, locked up for crimes he didn't commit, and threatened with mayhem everywhere he turns.

The problem with this kind of humor is that it wears thin very quickly. The jokes are obvious and not very funny, and the silly names become irritating after a while. It is obviou that O'Leary is going to get back to his own reality line eventually, so there is no real tension to the plot, and in fact there is not a whole lot of plot, just our hero going from one crisis to the next, each of which is virtually unrelated to the others. These were undoubtedly easy books to churn out, but far below the standards of Laumer's best work.

Time Trap (1970) opens with a series of time anomalies, people either displaced in time or caught in loops so that they repeat an endless cycle, even though they are aware that they have done the same things before. The story then focuses on Roger Tyson, who is down on his luck and who stumbles into the middle of a cross temporal battle. The potentially interesting story is undermined by Laumer's propensity for silliness. The usual episodic formula moves in fits and starts as he crosses from one time to another, dodging cave men, German artillery, and tentacled aliens. It turns out that they are all caught in a kind of multi-dimensional slide show whose owner is about to discard it, killing everyone inside as well as destroyingthe entire planet Earth, because of the alien infestation. Tyson has to thwart the aliens and convince the builder, a computer, to let the inhabitants survive. It has a few good moment, but only a few.

Deadfall (1971, filmed and re-released to tie in with the movie as *Fat Chance*, and the movie itself was renamed *Peeper*) is an homage to Raymond Chandler. Laumer does a reasonable pastiche although his plots and situations are so close to the original that they seem a bit too familiar. The story is a cross between *Farewell My Lovely* and *The Little Sister*. Joe Shaw is hired by an ex-crook to find the quasi-daughter he put up for adoption twenty five years earlier. He immediately links her to a wealthy and influential family, who bought the girl from the real adoptees for reasons never very clear. There is also a bunch of thugs after Shaw and his employer, both of whom get beaten up and knocked around a lot. He flirts with the women, his speech is full of colorful metaphors and rarely polite, and he has no respect for authority. A couple of murders later, he is no wiser about what is actually going on. The surprise revelation - the sister whom we are supposed to believe is the adopted girl is not and she is in fact the killer – is rather well done. This was a good enough novel that one might suspect that Laumer missed his calling, but it may be that he found it easier to churn out straightforward science fiction adventure stories rather than convoluted and more demanding mystery novels.   Although *The Star Treasure* (1971) also makes use of coincidence to advance the plot, it is less intrusive and for the most part this held together well. The protagonist discovers that the secret police are in command of the space navy in a future in which the solar system has been explored. At first he thinks it's just a local mutiny. Circumstances force him to escape back to Earth where he undergoes trials and tribulations, is pursued as a deserter and aided by an underground group he thinks are criminally insane, and eventually reaches the authorities, who promptly send him to a prison planet after convicting him of most of the crimes of which he was accused.

There he makes a place for himself and, despite having been railroaded by the authorities, he refuses to join the rebels. So he is troubled by both sides on an inhospitable planet. There is some political discussion, mostly about the tendency of rebels to replace one oligarchy or dictatorship with another rather than actually improve things. The end, alas, falls apart. He encounters aliens living secretly in the caves, aliens who give him a mental ability that allows him, within the course of a very few pages, to disarm the entire fleet and bring the secret rulers of Earth to their knees. A disappointing ending following a promising start.

Dinosaur Beach (1971) is an expansion of the shorter version, "The Time Sweepers." The protagonist is a time agent whose job is to prevent unauthorized tampering with history, a familiar and respected science fiction theme. Laumer's theory of time travel in this one is original, if not very sensible. The powers that be employ humanoid robots to change things in the past because since they are not alive, their activities cannot change the timestream. No, it doesn't make any sense to me either. Our hero goes from one crisis to another, largely without any act of volition of his own. Eventually he runs into a female agent, similarly stranded, although she may be from an alternate timeline. Female characters rarely have much to do in Laumer novels and this one is no exception although the chauvinism is relatively mild. This was one of Laumer's most disappointing books because it is quite well written up until the final third, during which he emulates A.E. van Vogt with lots of mumbo jumbo about time travel theory that just fills space and a rapid succession of revelations about higher and higher orders of civilization intervening in the past, the collapse of the universe, the discovery that the protagonist is an agent within an agent within an agent, and a few other odds and ends that turn it into an elaborate and unsatisfactory mishmash.

Retief of the CDT (1971) is another collection. The contents follow the same pattern as the earlier Retief adventures. "Ballots and Bandits" isn't bad. A planet newly freed from domination by the Groaci is having its first free elections, and Retief ends up as a candidate. "Mechanical Advantage" (aka "Retief, Long Awaited Master") is awful, however. Humans and Groaci quarrel over an apparently empty world in such an illogical manner that the story devolves into nonsense. Someone steals an entire building meant to impress the locals in "Pime Doesn't Cray", which is average.

"Internal Affairs" is better. A missing ambassador leads Retief to a gigantic intelligent creature who communicates with others by swallowing them. Finally, Retief has to mediate an end to an interplanetary war in the mediocre "The Piecemakers". A typical Retief collection varying from lightly amusing to annoyingly simpleminded. *Retief's Ransom* (1971) is more of the same except at greater length, set on a planet where the dominant species is a kind of gestalt of individual organs, limbs, etc. It is mildly amusing.

Lafayette O'Leary returned for his third adventure in *The Shape Changer* (1972). He had previously been confined to a single timeline but an old friend stumbles across some forbidden technology which O'Leary accidentally activates. He promptly finds himself in the unfamiliar body of a thief in a world very similar to the one he remembers, and is soon on the run from both the authorities and the tribe of thieves of whom he appears to be a member. There is also a jilted bride fond of knives and a thug with the same obsession, both with grudges against our hero. In flight, he stumbles upon another cave with another piece of forbidden technology and wakes up a mysterious man named Lom, who steals and apparently uses the device because O'Leary now finds himself in the body of a winged man capable of flight. And so it goes from that point on, with O'Leary traveling back and forth among bodies/realities until Laumer decided it had gone on long enough and tacked on a hasty and unconvincing ending.

Night of Delusions (1972) is more serious but no less chaotic. The protagonist agrees to be bodyguard for a high ranking politician who appears to have lost his mind. The man's associates want him to play along with the man's delusions - which involve aliens secretly invading Earth - hoping to shock him back to reality. Or are they actually trying to assassinate him and frame our hero? Neither explanation makes any sense within the context of the story. But their innocent dupe also begins to suffer multiple conflicting views of reality, suggesting that he might be the victim rather than the man he is supposed to be protecting. Just what is real and what is not? Every time he thinks he's beginning to understand, he finds himself back at an earlier point in the narrative. His own memories are intact, but those of everyone else have been changed, including a woman who is variously a stranger, a friend, and his wife.

Eventually he awakens in a laboratory where he is told that he was part of an experiment, but little more, and he cannot remember his past. Broke and confused, he encounters the woman from his dream and then discovers that the laboratory has disappeared, suggesting that perhaps this is still not the real world. A long succession of alternate realities and alternate explanations follow and at the end we still don't know what the "true" story is. The dreams within dreams device works for a while but by the end of the novel it has worn thin.

*The Infinite Cage (*1972) is surprisingly good given the trend of the previous several books. It even has a fairly complex plot and the characterizations are much better done than in almost anything else Laumer wrote. The protagonist is a thirty year old man who spent his entire life in an institution because he could not speak or function normally. He escapes and the author reveals that he is a natural telepath who has long been overwhelmed by all the voices he hears. After a period during which he assumes himself to be each of several other people based upon this contact, he begins to acquire sufficient knowledge and skills to get by in the world, although he never seems quite normal.

His superhuman powers don't always work to his benefit, however, and toward the end of the book he has lost his fortune, his "friends", and one leg. The conclusion is slightly muddled as he develops the power to regenerate the lost leg and cure his other problems, but then splits into two entities, one roughly human, the other a transcendent being that travels to the stars. Despite the disappointing ending, this is an excellent novel that suggests Laumer might have been a much more significant writer if he had devoted more effort to his work.

Time Tracks (1972) and *The Big Show* (1972) are both collections. The first opens with "The Timesweepers", which was expanded into the 1971 novel *Dinosaur Beach*. It is followed by a humorous fantasy, "The Devil You Don't," in which Lucifer comes to Earth to seek help in repelling an invasion by alien demons who have infiltrated hell. Although minor it is a lot funnier than most of Laumer's other efforts at comedy. "Mind Out of Time" is about an experimental star drive that allows people to somehow project themselves into alternate realities. The explanation makes little sense. "The Time Thieves" was collected earlier as "The Star-Sent Knaves" and "The Other Sky" is also a repeat.

The Big Show includes no previously collected stories, but none of those included are particularly notable. The first story is "In the Queue." It is somewhat atypical of Laumer, a satire about people standing in line for fifty years or so to have their papers processed, after which their lives are so empty that some of them get back in line. "A Relic of War" is a Bolo story. An aging machine adopted as a town mascot stirs to life when an old enemy killing machine is reactivated. This is the best story in the collection and arguably the best of the Bolo series. "The Big Show" is another satire of television addiction but lacking bite and quite silly. "Message to an Alien" has a single righteous man proving that the softies in the government who wanted to make peace with an alien enemy are wrong. The story is related to the novel *The Glory Game*. "The Plague" is a didactic political diatribe against do-gooders who force a landowner to accommodate a hoard of homeless people. It is clearly designed to prove the author's contention with little regard for what might actually happen in such a case. "Test to Destruction" is a murky tale of a dictatorship on Earth that is overthrown by a man aided by alien powers, which ultimately corrupt him as well.

The Glory Game (1973) is a prequel to and includes the short story, "Message to an Alien." It was one of Laumer's better written novels in many ways, but it is also a socio-political diatribe. It opens with Dalton, a maverick officer in the human space navy, explaining why it is okay for humans to exploit races technologically inferior to humanity, against the backdrop of an imminent war with the alien Hukks. Laumer then sets up his paper tiger. The softliners have decreed that the human fleet cannot fire upon the Hukks even if the latter attack them. This is such a ridiculous premise that it invalidates much of what follows.

Dalton is secretly told that he might destroy a few Hukks in the event of an attack if he does so before the admiral can order him not to fire. But the softliners also secretly give him orders authorizing him to relieve the admiral in order to anticipate an expected mutiny by hardliners. During the maneuver, Dalton detects a genuine attack aimed at Earth's moon, relieves the admiral, and initiates action against the Hukks. Laumer is somewhat balanced, however, and the hardliners are depicted as dishonorable, duplicitous, and cruel. After the surrender of the Hukk fleet, he derails a plan to annihilate the now virtually defenseless ships. Dalton is drummed out of the service after alienating both sides, but then saves the day again by preventing the invasion of a colony world. There is an attempt to balance viewpoints in this one, which is rare in polemic military fiction.

The Undefeated (1974) and *Retief: Emissary to the Stars* (1975) are both collections. The first repeats three stories from earlier volumes and only the fourth story, "Worldmaster" is new, while all four of the Retief stories are previously uncollected. The singleton is one of Laumer's better stories. In the aftermath of a major conventional war, a military commander decides to assume control of all of Earth, but after being opposed by one of his subordinates in a series of skirmishes, he realizes that he was acting unwisely and sabotages his own plot. The Retief formula is very outworn in those assembled here. "The Hoob Melon Crisis" has humans and Groaci contesting an uninhabited planet, with widespread stupidity on both sides. "The Garbage Invasion" is very similar, with the conflict this time involving whether or not it is okay for the Groaci to dump their garbage on another uninhabited world. "The Troubleshooter" and "The Negotiators" both involve thwarting Groaci takeover plans. It may have been that Laumer himself was getting tired of this series by now.

The Best of Keith Laumer (1976) and *Bolo* (1976) only collected three new stories between them. "Lawgiver" is a relatively even handed look at the battle between birth control and overpopulation, presenting arguments from both sides, and showing its impact on a politician who must decide whether or not to compromise his beliefs when he discovers his son has fathered a child about to be born illegally. "Field Test" involves a new model Bolo fighting machine that sacrifices itself in battle for the sake of honor. "The Last Command" is also a Bolo story. A pair of humans attempt to convince the programmed brain that its perception of their situation is incorrect, while the Bolo is convinced that they are actually enemy agents seeking to subvert its purpose.

The Ultimax Man (1972) was a pivotal point in Laumer's career because he experienced a debilitating stroke while writing it which resulted in physical and behavioral changes. The protagonist is a small time crook who is kidnapped by an alien who has been observing humans for centuries. In his hidden base, he begins to train his prisoner in every field of human endeavor, intellectual and physical, in order to test our racial potential and decide how humans should be approached by the rest of the universe. Except he isn't telling the whole truth, and the human does some sneaking around to acquire forbidden knowledge. It starts off reasonably well but Laumer could not resist the temptation to inject some farce. Eventually the human turns the tables on the alien, steals a ship and sets off to explore the galaxy, although he is quickly made a prisoner again. After drawing the reader through several sometimes confusing adventures, the author reveals that the aliens have been manipulating the human race for millennia, that there are superbeings on other worlds, but that none of them are able to stand up to a determined and aware human being.

Star Colony (1981) was supposed to be the first volume of a series, but the project never got beyond the first book. It is clumsy and awkward right from the opening sequences involving a crashlanding. Tensions among the crew and colonists start brewing and a secret alien observer has witnessed their arrival on what we but not the colonists know is an inhabited world. Eventually the humans meet the aliens, who are the most interesting element in the novel, but unfortunately not the real focus. The dialogue is stilted and the narrative disjointed and occasionally confusing. This was Laumer's longest novel, and in many ways his least interesting one. The characters are almost all interchangeable and they act in such an odd fashion that it is impossible to identify with them. Nor does Laumer make any real effort to show us the new planet.

Chrestomathy (1984) and *Once There Was a Giant* (1984) are both oddities. The first consists almost entirely of excerpts from previously published novels, plus two short stories, one of which had not been previously collected. "Birthday Party" is a very short piece in which the human life span is extended to five thousand years, but infancy is also multiplied by ten. The title story of the second book is a short novel that makes up half of the contents. It is one of Laumer's older stories involving a professional assassin coerced into arranging the death of the owner and sole inhabitant of a potentially valuable planet. His plan is to involve his target in a dangerous cross country journey during which he will hopefully die of natural causes, but during the course of their travels, he finds himself bonding to the strange man, who stands over ten feet tall. The second story is "No Ship Boots in Fairyland," which has a 1984 copyright but which is actually a slightly revised version of "The Other Sky" with a new title.

The Galaxy Builder (1984) is a Lafayette O'Leary story. The plot is a rehash of the earlier ones. Reality changes again and our hero has to find his way back to the world where he is happily married. The writing this time is more like the old Laumer, as is the plot which moves from one episode to the next at a hectic pace. The characters resemble the unsophisticated comic aliens from the Retief stories and the humor is much the same, based on silly accidents, dumb misunderstandings, and convenient coincidences. O'Leary is sentenced to death for a crime he doesn't recall having committed, which supposedly caused a discontinuity in space and time. He is into and out of dungeons regularly as he tries to figure out what happened and change things back to the way they were previously. Half way through, O'Leary realizes that the ongoing changes are not random, that he is being manipulated by person or persons unknown. A variety of nonsense follows before he traces the people responsible and, after apparently being separated from the reality he seeks forever, is finally reinstated.

Laumer returned to familiar ground with *Retief to the Rescue* (1983) and *The Return of Retief* (1984), both very much in the style of the earlier stories. Since this series was never among Laumer's more ambitious efforts, the two new novels are rather disappointing. In the first, Retief is caught between the Creepies and the Crawlies, two subsets of a local native species involved in a rather peculiar war which seems to target Terran embassy officials rather more than could be pure chance. The Groaci are around to stir things up as well, but in a very subsidiary way. The second one is much less interesting. Another alien race begins to encroach on human space and naturally the diplomatic corps is incompetent and seems likely to aid the invaders rather than the humans, until Retief singlehandedly finds a way to turn the tide against the bad guys.

End As a Hero (1985) is an expansion of the short story of the same name. Humans are at war with the alien Gool, who use their telepathic powers to implant hallucinations in the minds of the crew of Terran ships, leading to mutiny, assassination, and general chaos.

The protagonist not only survives one of these attacks but the contact enables him to learn the secret of telepathic spying and he is therefore able to discover the Gool secrets and the methods by which they can be defeated. Unfortunately, it is known that he was in contact with them and since no one else has managed to survive with an intact mind, the authorities on Earth believe that he is a saboteur and decide to kill him rather than listen to him. The extended version manages to avoid some of the internal contradictions of the original story and holds together much better.

Rogue Bolo (1986) is almost an epistolary novel, consisting of very short fragments of conversations, news reports, and thought streams mixed with more conventional narrative. The Mark XXX bolo is self aware and self programming and very controversial because it is virtually unstoppable. Why a unified world government would build one is never really explained given the absence of enemies. The new weapon promptly begins acting outside the parameters expected by its creators. This is because it is able to perceive threats invisible to human eyes, including terrorists and a hostile alien force lurking on the outskirts of the solar system. The prose is awkward, it is badly plotted, poorly thought out, and ultimately dull.

Retief and the Pangalactic Pageant of Pulchritude (1986, an expansion of *Retief's Ransom*) and *Reward for Retief* (1989) are both negligible. Added to the original story in the first is Retief's stint as judge at an interstellar beauty pageant and the consequences thereof. The second is entirely new but says nothing innovative. Reticf is assigned to a planet of intelligent caterpillars who are clearly anti-Terran and clearly plotting something nefarious. Laumer moves this series toward the Lafayette O'Leary universe by creating a nexus of alternate worlds in which our hero finds himself temporarily lost until, naturally, he solves all the problems and outsmarts the natives, but is given no credit by his superiors. This was the weakest of the Retief novels and Laumer's worst novel since *Catastrophe Planet*.

Retief returned yet again in *Retief in the Ruins* (1986), which follows the usual pattern. The bulk of the book consists of the title novella, in which humans and Groaci are contending for the technical secrets of an alien race which is in serious decline but which once was a dominating force in the galaxy. As usual, Retief works around his bumbling superiors and solves the problem on his own terms. There are two long stories included, both also featuring Retief. "There Is a Tide" is quite similar, revolving around a plan to develop the ecology of another contested planet. The third story is "The Woomy." This time the Groaci are trying to tie up the timber export business on a forest planet, but Retief foils them as usual.

The Stars Must Wait (1990) follows the adventures of a space pilot who awakens from an inadvertent one hundred year suspended animation to find himself in a future where Bolos, quasi-intelligent tanks, have begun to experience systemic malfunctions. It's a massive rewrite and expansion of "Night of the Trolls". The hero discovers that Earth has descended into a feudal state and a local baron is using the threat of a functional bolo under his control to keep the locals in line. The protagonist upsets the order of things, removes the bolo threat, and overthrows the baron after persevering despite a variety of difficulties. One of the best of his latest novels, although obviously a retread of ideas he developed years earlier.

Zone Yellow (1990) is an Imperium novel featuring Brion Bayard. This series had gone steadily downhill from the outset and this installment hits bottom. Bayard has to find the timeline of origin of a race of intelligent rats who are invading the other realities and spreading a deadly plague. Although the background resembles the earlier books in the serie, the tone is very different and Bayard doesn't seem like the same person at all.

Judson's Eden (1991), *Back to the Time Trap* (1992), and *Retief and the Rascals* (1993) were Laumer's final three novels. The first one is a standalone that has a clever concept and deals with it reasonably well. A wealthy man flees from the rapacious government of Earth but crashes on a planet where time doesn't work in the same linear fashion as it does elsewhere in the universe. Eventually he begins to understand at least part of the laws of nature there, enough that he is able to take advantage of them when the evil government people track him down. The cardboard characters detract from what might otherwise have been a considerably better book.

Back to the Time Trap is the second and final adventure of Roger Tyson. Two alien races with godlike powers are battling to control all of space and time and Tyson gets caught in the middle for a succession of sometimes amusing anomalies and dilemmas. The final Retief novel is tolerable but it offers absolutely nothing new and simply retreads the same battle with the Groaci for influence with stupid alien indigenes plot that Laumer had already used a score or more times previously.

The last few collections have a handful of previously unreprinted stories. In *The Long Twilight and Other Stories* (2008) there is "The Half Man." It's a more serious story than most of Laumer's shorts. In a future when humans have altered their own DNA to diversify and populate otherwise unwelcoming worlds, a half breed finds his destiny on a planet where humans have reverted to living underwater. "Of Death What Dreams" can be found in *A Plague of Demons & Other Stories* (2003). It's a dystopian story that ends with alien contact and is written with dialogue using lots of innovative idioms that actually get rather annoying by the end, although the story is otherwise not bad at all. "The Secret", in *Retief: Diplomat at Arms* (1982) is a standard and minor Retief story. "Three Blind Mice" is in *Legions of Space* (2004). Three humans crash on an ice world where snow blindness is virtually inevitable, pursued by inimical aliens who want to kill any human who observes one of their ships. This is one of Laumer's best short stories. There are two more in *Alien Minds* (1991). "Reverse English" is a very short extended gimmick story about outsmarting a rogue computer. "The Propitiation of Brullamagoo" is a novelette that can best be described as a Retief story without Retief.

There are several Laumer stories that remain uncollected as of this writing. Probably the most interesting of these is "Diplomat-at-Arms", the very first Retief story from January 1956 *Fantastic*, which is totally different from all of those which followed. Retief is an old man, his superior, Magnan, is reasonable, there is no mention of the Groaci, and no humor at all. "Street Scene" is a humorous piece written in collaboration with Harlan Ellison which opens with an impossibly large pteranodon crashing into a city street. I recommend reading this in Ellison's collection *Partners in Wonder* because there are two different endings and this is the only place where both are provided. The remaining stories are all very minor. "The Choice" (July 1969 *Analog*) is a mildly humorous piece about space explorers taken captive by a superintelligent artifact. "The Soul Buyer" (December 1963 *Fantastic*) is related to "The Other Sky" in that it involves the secret invasion of Earth by the Niss, although this one is set way before the events in the better known story. "Stranger in Paradox" (August 1961 *Fantastic*) involves escaping from a prison planet. "Rank Injustice", from *New Destinies*, is a minor Retief story. Finally we have two related stories that appear together in *The Best from If* (1973), "The Right to Revolt" and "The Right to Resist." In the first, colonists on a planet run by a corporation rebel rather than accept the imposition of new colonists and the pre-emptive relocations of those already in place. In the second, the rebels have taken over but now face unrest from the people they rule. Both tend to lecture rather than show.

There are a number of other Laumer collections that just reshuffle the stories already mentioned above. These include *Retief Unbound* (1979), *Retief at Large* (1978), *Knight of Delusions* (1982), *The Complete Bolo* (1990), *Retief!* (2001), *Odyssey* (2002), and *Future Imperfect* (2003). Laumer was very consistent throughout his career, both his good points and the bad ones. Although he never had a breakout novel, this was probably in large part because of his reluctance to take on serious themes in a serious manner. The first halves of most of his novels are almost always engaging and entertaining, but he seems not to have had a clear goal in mind and his use of coincidence and shallow characterization almost always limited the effectiveness of his book length work.

ARCHITECTS OF TOMORROW
D.G. COMPTON

British author D.G. Compton's first science fiction novel, *The Quality of Mercy*, appeared in the UK in 1965 but wasn't available to the US public until a revised edition appeared in 1970 following the success of his later work. I've never seen the British version, but I'd suspect that the anti-American sentiments expressed were toned down as part of the revision. Compton doesn't single out the Americans for rebuke. The Chinese and Russians are portrayed as equally culpable, and the protagonist – who is British – is perhaps even guiltier because he knows what he is doing.

This is a Cold War novel, and as such it is pretty dated politically as well as scientifically, which is rather a shame because the sentiments and concerns are as relevant as ever, perhaps more so. Simply stated, US and British pilots are conducting secret aerial missions over the Communist bloc, taking advantage of a hole in their radar coverage, spraying radioactive particles that serve some vague monitoring purpose, or at least so we are told. Presumably the other side is doing the same because the spread of a mysterious, deadly disease known as VPD has spread over the entire world, and most of the population – along with the reader – knows that it is somehow caused by radioactivity. It is neither contagious nor infectious, so the victims mix freely in society, although we soon learn that the establishment is taking steps to keep those affected out of the public eye.

Our protagonist is Donald Morrison, a priggish, inhibited sort who works with the Americans on one of the aircraft. He and his wife live in a special compound where they are granted all the luxuries that are in short supply elsewhere, after enormous waves of immigration have made it impossible to maintain the former standard of living (this is supposedly set in 1979). Since the air crews are predominantly male, there is a disproportionately large number of nurses, who are obviously there to satisfy the sexual needs of the servicemen, who are discouraged from fraternizing with the locals. The aircraft are called Peace Probe Bombers, an evident contradiction in terms.

The government, which has been in power for twenty seven years without a break, has become increasingly repressive. People are encouraged to inform on one another, and Morrison does that very thing very early on. There are other signs of the collapse of human society. The arts are in a serious decline and people have lost faith in their leaders. Although there is a test ban treaty in effect, no one has any faith in it, and the more than two million VPD victims testify to its ineffectiveness. The populace is increasingly alienated and dehumanized. "One was tabulated down to the last eyeblink." A policy of cultural nationalism has been imposed. The traditions and social activities of every population of 50,000 or more are imposed by law, so that London television programs cannot be shown in Bristol, for example. The suicide rate is climbing and some tall buildings are secured to prevent people from publicly and spectacularly expressing their final protest.

On some level, Morrison knows that his superiors are lying to him, that the spraying is related to the new plague, and that he is personally responsible for an unknown number of deaths. When one of his colleagues wavers, the cover story is that he had a crisis of conscience, but Morrison knows this is also a lie. This further undermines his ability to ignore what is happening around him. "But if we can't trust them, who can we trust?" The command structure is frequently referred to as "godlike" or in other religious terms such as being like a "serpent". Morrison also recognizes that he is losing himself, that he is assuming different personalities for different situations. "How many people was he?" He and his wife abide in relative peace, even when their estrangement begins, because it just isn't done to be emotional. Moods are okay, but only "in moderation". It would never do to make a scene. During one mission, Morrison recognizes that he "was an appendage of a computer program." A bit later, his wife tells him that he's getting "just like one of his computers." He has trouble differentiating among the wives of his colleagues, who seem to him uniform in their perfection.

He doesn't begin to acknowledge this until he is confronted by a group of protesters who want him to carry a fatally ill woman to a hospital. Knowing that there is no treatment available, and not wanting to expose his wife to the reality around them, he refuses, and has to use tear gas to avoid a violent confrontation. Paradoxically, the teargas has an adverse on the woman's condition and she dies, this time undeniably as a result of his actions, precipitating a violent demonstration at the airbase, alienation between Morrison and his wife, and his desire to wash his hands of it all and resign. His ability to resist the truth is further eroded by the presence of an old friend, the Squadron Leader, who apparently knows more than he should about what is really going on at the airbase. Nevertheless, he is convinced that it is his friend who is irrational, distanced from the world. "Madness is a disease of separation."

Morrison concludes that "The ultimate responsibility could be put on nobody, because this is a democracy." That is a two bladed sword because in one sense, it is literally true. We are complicit in the decisions of the government we elect; we cannot separate "them" from "us". But it is also effectively a fallacy, because the government has effectively changed the electorate into a fragmented, regimented, mass who for the most part no longer believe that their desires have any impact on the course of events. The populace at large is not responsible because it can't be, and it can't be responsible because it isn't.

Morrison also acknowledges that he is subject to a generalized feeling of guilt, but feels that it is universal, perhaps correctly although he has a particularly rich justification for it. He is hardly even bothered when he discovers that his mail is being read, and on some level he realizes that he would have been surprised to learn otherwise. The news that the now absent military officer is being held incommunicado, supposedly following a breakdown, doesn't seem to bother him either. His growing unrest is partially soothed by an encounter with the captain of the fencing team, an "impeccably controlled man". Control has now become the single most important thing in Morrison's life, and he knows that he is losing it.

That loss of control eventually leads to a dalliance with a nurse, although he tries to justify it to himself as a burden on his soul and no affront to his wife, just as he has previously tried to justify his job for the military. The incident becomes another convoluted lie, reinterpreted by the staff psychologist as an innocent trip to visit the father of the dead girl. Morrison now realizes at least in part the extent to which his life is being watched, but apparently remains unaware that there is a camera monitoring his activities, even in his own bedroom.

Morrison is perhaps unsalvageable. When the Squadron Leader finally confronts him with the truth, that the three megapowers are cooperatively wiping out one fifth of the population of the Earth in order to ease the population pressure, he shoots his old friend through the head. The source of his information, a civilian employee, is retained because he is "rather like a computer" and can be effectively convinced to believe a new program. He and his commanding officer agree that they had a right, if not an obligation, to protect themselves and society from "truths" that are uncomfortable, tacitly accepting that the border between truth and lie has become hopelessly smudged. He fails to convince his wife, who leaves him, that it is alright sometimes to "adjust reality", to believe what you want to believe rather than what is really the case. Then he reveals that on some level he has always known the truth, insisting that she can't leave him, that "they" won't let her do so because it would affect his morale. But in this he is wrong. And his ultimate betrayal comes when he agrees to sign the papers committing her to an institution. This is a novel designed to depress and alarm the reader about the way in which we, as individuals and as a society, allow ourselves to become inured to the increasingly inhuman ways in which we treat one another.

The Silent Multitude (1966) is in part a commentary on the way in which we let artificial things, artifacts, and coldly functional environments affect how we feel and what we think. The opening viewpoint character is a cat prowling through an almost deserted cathedral in Gloucester, and although we are not told explicitly until later what has been happening, we already have a sense that the city is nearly deserted and that something terrible is in progress. The theme is well established in the opening sequence. The pigeons living in the cathedral are so used to being fed by the congregation that they have had no experience with natural food and are unable to forage for themselves. The cat is prevented from pouncing on its natural prey – a cluster of sparrows – because they have taken refuge in a Christmas tree which is so laden with lights and ornaments that it is impossible to climb. The cat, prowling the city, explores a house which it finds uninteresting because it "contained no animals". The lone human figure, the Dean of Gloucester, has reached a point in life when he is unable to separate the physical existence of the cathedral from his belief in God. So Compton has demonstrated that physical constructs, or perhaps civilization itself, has separated us from the natural world, the spiritual world, and perhaps even from the means of sustaining life.

We then revert three days backward, when the still unspecified crisis was looming but had not reached the point of precipitating panicky flight from the city. Compton shows us a nondescript man in "plasticized gray flannel" as he moves through a crowd that doesn't even note his existence. The fact that it is Christmas season – the time when we are more concerned about purchasing or receiving things than enjoying one another – is hardly coincidental. The man is Paper Smith, a recluse who lives secretly – or so he thinks – in the abandoned ground floor of a corporate center. His presence is tolerated and he is looked upon favorably by several taxi drivers, but his life never meaningfully intersects with that of anyone else. Smith encounters a stranger in the park, a man who clearly feels guilt about having put his elderly father in a nursing facility, a place that is "steel-lined" and sheltered/isolated from the outside world.

The reclusive Smith knows something is up, but it doesn't really impinge on his world. Compton does divulge its name, the Falling Sickness, but provides no details until midway through the novel. Smith pays a daily visit to the museum where he spends hours watching landscapes and seascapes, but skims through "constructions, abstracts, dyed expanded polystyrene" and other non-representational art. The people he meets are all living in what is effectively another world, an orderly place with hierarchies of authority, rules of conduct, and standard procedures. "Without consistency bank managers suffocate." When Smith finds the tea dispensing machine shut down, he falls against it and is literally supported by its existence, retreats into abject panic when it does not function as it should. Even he, living on the fringe of society, cannot escape his conditioning.

Smith is one of a few people who evade the mandatory evacuation. As he prowls about in the aftermath, he notices a stainless steel model of the inside of a human mouth, which he views as "obscene", reminding us of the disparity between real and artificial, and later he becomes fascinated by a display of artificial flowers. He meets a news photographer named Sally Paget who is photographing the last hours of the city, but she sees him as an element in a photographic composition, not as a person. Her name is possibly significant as Paget's disease is a virus that attacks the bones, the infrastructure of the body, where, as we eventually learn, the Falling Sickness is a fungus from outer space which attacks concrete, the infrastructure of cities. Photojournalists recur as significant characters in some of Compton's later novels. Back at the cathedral, the Dean muses about "lifelong constructions of relative importance" and notes that his housekeeper "openly despised gadgets". He knows her by the services she performed rather than the person she was. He is subsequently soothed by the organized layout of the city which offers a place for "minds rather than bodies", intellect rather than emotion.

Smith and Paget run into Simeon, a man who follows the Falling Sickness from city to city because he enjoys seeing them crumble into ruin. His name may be a reference to the Biblical Simeon, whose tribe was condemned to wander from place to place as punishment for a past crime. This linkage is further confirmed when he attempts to rape Paget, as the Biblical Simeon raped Dinah. They are joined in due course by the Dean, who reveals that Simeon's father was the head architect for the recent redesign of Gloucester. Simeon contends that modern civilization is like a drug, and its inhabitants all addicts. He characterizes the city his father helped build as a monster. The Dean's confusion of God with the cathedral is repeated several times, and when the police return to the doomed city searching for Paget, the author tells us "They were human beings really, catching machinery like a disease." Paget in turns thinks of herself as a slot machine "dispensing instant analysis" while Simeon refuses to admit even to himself that society is composed of people, believing it instead to be an artificial creation separate from humanity.

As the collapses proliferate, the Cathedral remains standing although Sims insists the only thing holding it together is the "weight of its own inertia", a statement both literally and perhaps metaphorically true. One is left with the conviction that for Compton, the destruction of the city is not entirely a bad thing because it severs humanity's enslavement to the artificial. The devouring fungus is referred to within the book as a silent multitude, but the term also applies to the mass of people who surrender to the strictures of society without protest. Gloucester is standing in for the Biblical Jericho, of course, the city which came "tumbling down".

Joshua's curse was that the builder of Jericho would lose his son, and Simeon – son of the head architect – is killed by Paget during the attempted rape.

The tone of the novel is, on the surface, of gloom and decay. Smith at one point summarizes life succinctly: "Eating and going to the toilet – what else is there when you come down to it?" It ends, however, on a more hopeful note, despite the demise of Simeon, who clearly had a death wish from the outset. Smith survives against all expectations, and even has better prospects for the future because of the revelation that his late wife left behind a substantial fortune. Paget gets her story and discovers the ability to empathize with others which she had previously suppressed. The Dean survives the collapse of the cathedral without losing his faith. And perhaps the world that must evolve out of the spreading collapse will be a softer, more human environment.

It may be useful to speculate about the title. The only poem quoted in the book is by Sylvia Plath, but it seems likely that Compton must have been familiar with "Silent Multitude" by the early 19th Century poet, Mrs. Hemans. The poem opens with a reference to a "mighty and a mingled throng gathered in one spot", obviously a city. She goes on to speculate that what causes the multitudes to be silent is the fear of death, and that we are in one sense always alone because we must face that ultimate fear by ourselves. Each of the characters in Compton's story intends to face their possible death in the crumbling city alone, and it is only through happenstance that the four are brought together.

Farewell, Earth's Bliss (1966) opens aboard a shuttle carrying twenty four deportees to a penal colony on Mars. They are all drugged to keep them manageable during the flight and each has been assigned a new name, all drawn from the Bible, apparently as a symbol of the life they are to lead. The colony has existed for twelve years and has about two hundred residents, but neither the newcomers nor the reader learns much more about it during the early chapters. There are open comparisons to the founding of this colony as a new Canaan and there are religious references throughout.

Each of several characters is sketched in, some more thoroughly than others. Joshua, for example, is troubled by the formlessness of the future. "Wherever you are, you need shape." Ruth is determined to overcome whatever adversity comes. "The exercise of her humanity was precious to her." Simon shows signs of mild aggression despite the drugs, and we learn that he had an unsavory reputation when he was known as Thornton Clare, who burned a black man to death. Mark feels driven to take charge, as best he can, and worries about potential trouble makers. He views Simon as a rival and when he intercedes on the half of Jacob, who is black, his contempt and patronizing tone make Jacob resent him even more than he does Simon. We pick up bits and pieces about the others. Ruth is a psychologist; Mark was deported after a failed assassination attempt. Compton also suggests that their altered circumstances have general as well as specific psychological effects. While discussing racing pigeons, among whom there is virtually no sex drive, Ruth comments that "captivity does that to a lot of animals". But the situation changes quickly when they finally arrive on Mars.

    Compton's Mars isn't far from what we now know to be reality. It is barren and the atmosphere will not support human life. There is some life on Mars, mostly lichens, but no intelligent creatures. There are also sandstorms which last for weeks, and a lengthy one starts shortly after their arrival. Although they have had a visit from the senior colonists, they are still confined to the ship, and when they are cut off by the storm, fifteen of their number starve to death before the storm subsides. The survivors face what is clearly a repressive society where Preventive Hunger, i.e. withholding of rations, is a common form of punishment, where the new names assigned to them are dropped after a period of one year, and where many of the things they were told to expect just do not exist.

    We begin to see the true nature of the colony very quickly. Despite the apparent kindness of the families who take in the survivors, there is steel beneath the velvet. Those who put others at risk are executed by exposure. Unsatisfactory performance of one's job leads to Preventive Hunger. There is even a suggestion that the established colonists may have known of the sandstorm in advance and used it to winnow out the weaker newcomers. Ruth is accused of sedition, of corrupting children, and disappears apparently to avoid execution, but she is actually the secret mistress of the governor. The newcomers eventually learn that, contrary to what they believed, there is no two way communication with Earth. They are dumped and left, out of sight and out of mind.

At the same time, the religious undertones become more prominent. Paul seems to be hallucinating about seeing the ice catch fire, comparing it to the burning bush of the Bible, and before long others witness the phenomenon, unparalleled in their experience. The exiles compare themselves to the Semites. We are told that the church was founded on "blindness, loneliness, and fear" and it is not surprising that the new religion growing among the exiles values ignorance and considers knowledge a sin. At the same time, it is an inadequate solace for some, particularly Jacob who takes his troubles to the rector and leaves worse off than when he came.

The novel never quite pulls together. There is no central story and no resolution to the subplots of the individual characters. Their new society is repulsive and probably doomed to ultimate failure. It suggests the inadequacy of religion to sustain us, but suggests that the miraculous is possible. Despite some very effective scenes, the novel is too unfocused to be effective.

Synthajoy (1968) is another story entirely, no pun intended. It opens with a woman locked in some undefined mental institution. She was at one time married to the man who invented Synthajoy, a way to record and playback the emotional states of people to be experienced vicariously by others. Thea Cadence was no longer in love with her husband, Edward, and in fact was having an affair with one of his associates, Tony Stech. The novel alternates scenes during her confinement with flashbacks to the history of the development of the technology.

In the early stages, her husband at least professed to be motivated by a desire to help humanity. People who were sexually dysfunctional could begin to heal if they experienced genuine, conventional sex as recorded by another couple. Even at that point, however, Thea seems to have suspected that he had other motives as well.

One of the flashbacks is to Thea's early encounters with Stech, whose father died while under Dr. Cadence's care because he had lost the will to live rather than from any physical cause. When he berates her for their inability to help, she suggests that it may not have been the best course of action to "cure" his father even if that had been possible, that maybe he was happiest having made his decision. "Do we have to attack him with mechanisms?" she asks, or should they just let nature take its course. Stech, however believes "in the pain of staying alive." This segues into the opening of a subtle argument, which would be repeated in different form in Compton's subsequent work. Does the fact that we know how to accomplish something technologically mean that we should actually do it, and, if we take some of those elements which make an individual unique and share them with large numbers of people, are we depriving both donors and receivers of the right to be themselves, however limited or imperfect?

Naturally the good intentions which were touted at first have become perverted. Thea is herself being subjected to a tape of a man in abject contrition as part of her treatment for having committed some as yet unspecified act of aggression. She also believes that while they insist she is receiving contrition, they are actually filling her with guilt, which we subsequently learn is true, though whether at the discretion of the doctor or whether it is part of a secret agenda the secret agenda of the court is unresolved. The conversations between Thea and her doctor resemble the arguments in Orwell's *Nineteen Eighty-Four*, reflecting conflicting views of reality.

Thea's relationship with both the doctor and her assigned nurse, is ambiguous. The nurse appears sympathetic but Thea suspects this may be part of the treatment. The doctor strikes her on one occasion, which suggests that something out of the ordinary might be going on. This is all reinforced by flashbacks to her trial, for the murder of her husband following the suicide of her lover. It is evident that she was found insane for political rather than judicial reasons and that the testimony against her was tainted and the judge prejudiced. We also discover that the tapes are addictive and that Dr. Cadence had in fact bowed to coercion and given a criminal organization the exclusive rights to distribute the tapes.

Compton addresses the problem of scientific advance through the words of Tony Stech. "We can't choose where to stop, what to discover and what's better left unknown." We see the same ethical questions rising now with regard to cloning, genetic engineering, and stem cell experimentation. The only advocacy for the value of the discovery is Stech, who isn't sure that he believes his own statements, which robs the story of some of its potential, but it still makes a strong argument for protecting the individual against homogenization. The ending is also ambiguous. Thea apparently did kill her husband despite her memories that it was his mistress who was responsible. She also seems to have altered her stance and now plans to further her husband's researches as soon as she is released. This suggests that Compton was pessimistic about the future of technology.

The Steel Crocodile (1970, aka *The Electric Crocodile*) is set in a future England where there has evolved a strange balance between the right of privacy and government surveillance. Although the government is allowed to use tracking devices and other technology to keep track of people of interest, individuals have the right to destroy the devices and evade detection. The protagonist, Matthew Oliver, is approached by Gryphon, an old acquaintance who wants him to accept a job at the Colindale Institute so that he can spy on them. The Institute's activities are somewhat mysterious and they are suspected of using subtle forms of control to influence the shape of scientific development. Oliver is of two minds on the subject, particularly after his acquaintance is murdered within hours of their conversation. The polarization of society is so pronounced that Abigail, Matthew's wife, theorizes that Gryphon was murdered because of his "moderation" rather than because of some overt act he committed.

They move to the institute, which provides housing. Almost immediately they learn that Oliver's predecessor, Henderson, died in a burning car and that it was not an accident, although the intended victim was possibly the head of the institute, not Henderson, who just happened to borrow his car. Matthew learns the purpose of the institute, which is to repress certain scientific advances and encourage others in what the staff believes is the most beneficial way for the human race. Within that elite lies another, a select group which is using their sophisticated computer to try to design a new religion that will resonate in modern times. This last fact is a reflection of the major conflict in the novel, which is between Matthew and Abigail. Abigail believes in God, but Matthew recognizes that he does not, but that he wishes that he could believe in one.

The computer itself becomes his rationalized deity, a being which disinterestedly directs humanity for its own good. Although Abigail never learns of the plans to create a new religion, she is appalled by the arrogance of those attempting to decide all important issues in a star chamber atmosphere and by the lack of privacy for employees who live with microphones in every room of their homes and who cannot go out without notifying their "tail", a security person assigned to monitor their every action. Matthew considers all of this a small sacrifice in return for the privilege of participating in such great events, to be so close to the godhead. Matthew himself tends to make every decision, even in trivial matters, somehow appear to be a moral choice.

The title refers to a model of a crocodile head which is supposed to signify the unfettered advance of science, devouring every bit of knowledge in its path without regard to the consequences. Compton does provide examples of the untoward effects of progress. Increased longevity has led to new mental illnesses including a kind of terminal depression in which people feel they have overstayed their welcome. This and other factors have created a gaping generation gap, and given rise not only to semi-official resistance movements but even a more active one of which Abigail's brother is secretly a member. There is also an entire class of people who are termed "alienees", so alienated from society that they are formally disenfranchised. Disagreement with the status quo is considered a form of schizophrenia, and Abigail's resistance is diagnosed as such in the waning chapters, resulting in her imprisonment.

The computer, which supposedly just finds associations among disparate facts, actually extrapolates from them, identifying potential outcomes. The head of Colindale suggests that this is the creative process in humans, and therefore the computer has become a creator. He also justifies the secrecy of the process. "People in a democracy don't like being told what is good for them." Since the computer is the product of the human mind, he sees no problem with allowing the computer to direct human destiny, since its source was human. Although sabotage eventually destroys the computer, it is clear that this is a temporary reprieve and that another one will be built and the process will continue.

Compton's disenchantment with humanity is demonstrated again in Matthew's relationship with Abigail. As was the case with the protagonist of *The Quality of Mercy*, he believes that her incarceration might be best because the importance of the work in which he is engaged overrides questions of personal rights or loyalties. Once again we are shown people abdicating the responsibility to manage their own lives. Even as Matthew accepts the right to decide for people as a whole, he is surrendering that right to the computer. In many ways the novel is very similar to *The Quality of Mercy*, differing only in the nature of the threat. Readers might be amused at Compton's now outdated view of computer operations – they use tape readers and line printers – but they are not likely to be amused by the implications.

The Chronocules (1970, aka *Hot Wireless Sets, Aspirin Tablets, the Sandpaper Sides of Used Matches, and Something That Might Have Been Castor Oil*) involves another secretive scientific installation. This one is in a small town in England where a mysterious, indestructible book has appeared. It was first seen by a mentally ill young man named Roses who later functions as the village idiot, part of the installation's camouflage. David Silberstein is the administrator although the site was founded by Manny Littlejohn for reasons which are not immediately revealed. Part of the complement is a team of athletically developed men and women who are, obviously, meant to spearhead some dangerous experiment at some point.

The degree to which Silberstein, and by extension the entire facility, is divorced from the natural world is illustrated when he notices Roses fishing with a hook and line, which strikes him as anachronistic since there is equipment available which could harvest every fish in the area effortlessly within a few moments. One of the other characters observes that it is entirely possible that in his entire life, David Silberstein never once had any fun. Indeed, we discover that one of the prerequisites for being chosen to work on this project is a psychological as well as a physical separation from the outside world.

We don't see much of that world, although we are told that it is succumbing to pollution, overpopulation, and other woes. There is no serious evidence of that dissolution inside the project, other than an almost clinically casual attitude toward sex, presumably a reflection of the collapsing moral values of the outside world. We do, however, discover the purpose of the project, which is intended to develop time travel so that the participants can escape to a presumably better world or time. The experiments have not been going well, however. Although they can move items outside the normal time stream, when they return the shock of arrival inevitably destroys them, making human travel clearly impossible. One of the scientists, Liza, considers the possibility that they are abdicating their responsibility to the present by running rather than fighting, but she is not troubled enough to seriously consider leaving.

The man leading the project is a ruthless megalomaniac who orders the execution of several people for trivial reasons during the course of the novel. Eventually the outside world overcomes their barriers, however. An inspector is sent in who is just as reprehensible as the director, and through misrepresentation and misunderstanding she precipitates a crisis involving government intervention, a riot in the adjacent town, and the destruction of the project. There is, however, one successful transmission and the time traveler is met in the future by the now much older Liza, who initially appears to be something of a hero, only to reveal that over the course of time she has been corrupted into a close copy of the tyrant who ran the operation in the first place. A relentlessly depressing, though fascinating novel which questions the ways in which science sometimes pursues issues independently of the human factor, while also pointing out the almost fanatical fear of science that dominates some parts of our culture. There are really no heroes in this one, and the villains are us.

Compton's next was *The Missionaries* (1972), only slightly less downbeat in tone. A team of four alien missionaries arrives on Earth. Part of their protocol is to capture two of the local indigenes – humans in this case – in order to evaluate the task of conveying their mystical revelations to a new species. They land near a small town in Devon, where a college student named Dacre Wordsworth is awaiting the presumed imminent death of his father, a career military officer, with mixed emotions. Dacre is also head of a small motorcycle gang and acts as a restraining influence on their frequently anarchistic inclinations. His mother refuses to accept her husband's condition and is unrelentingly critical of her son's lifestyle. He and a casual girlfriend, Janey, are riding alone one night when they are chosen to be specimens.

The missionaries release them, but they have shaped the experience to conform to a pre-existing scenario in the minds of the two humans, who subsequently believe that they were interrogated by Russian spies, improbable as that idea may be. Government officials however, have noticed the unusual aerial phenomena and they are combing the moors with military forces. The missionaries appear at the Wordsworth house the following morning, having taken on the appearance of four young bikers. The Wordsworths easily see through their cover story, so the foursome admit the truth, or part of it, and one of them intervenes to help cure the elder Wordsworth's emphysema, despite the protestations of his wife, who considers their actions indecent.

Mrs. Wordsworth undergoes an immediate transformation when her husband's life is saved, recognizing that much of what she believed was false, that she never really believed in Christianity in the first place, just gave it lip service. She is now ready to accept the existence of the god of the missionaries, Ustiliath, which exists in all energy, performs miracles, but is unknowable. "God was the lie of her life." Mr. Wordsworth, paradoxically, is not happy at first to be cured, since it has upset the established order of his life.

Dacre, meanwhile, remains highly skeptical, particularly when one of the missionaries suggests that his mother's conversion may have been premature and therefore unhelpful. Their arguments are simplistic. Instead of good and evil, they suggest constructive and destructive, and since the universe exists, then obviously the former must have won. The easy conversion of Mrs. Wordsworth and a casual visitor, Wilcox, are not entirely plausible, although it is possible that the author intended this as an example of how Christian missionaries judged as successes the impulsive actions of their assumed converts.

The cured elder Wordsworth has ambivalent thoughts and almost turns his visitors in to the authorities. While he recognizes that his wife did not understand her old faith and therefore feels no need to understand the new, he requires a deeper comprehension and a purpose in life. He cannot accept that his health was restored as a gift, without any expected recompense. At a minimum, if it was miraculous, he feels obligated to find a new purpose in life, a reason why he has been thus chosen. Human nature being what it is, Mrs. Wordsworth and Wilcox both decide to ignore their instructions and try to bring about conversions, and both fail miserably and in different ways. Her essential uncertainty and shallowness of thought fail to convince the local priest, and his bad temper and poor judgment alienate a crowd that gathers when he tries to harangue them in public.

The situation changes dramatically within a few pages. One of

Dacre's gang members stabs Wilcox, then hangs himself in an abandoned building. Mrs. Wordsworth admits that there are strangers at the house and one of the police officers who arrive is killed by some mysterious mental force used by the missionaries, although they immediately surrender and the death is not attributed to them. Dacre is also puzzled by their references to their "necessary machines", a relationship they won't explain. They also state that their religion, like all religions, is utilitarian, striving for the betterment of its followers, but there appears to be a cold, analytical, even inhuman undertone to their words. He accuses the missionaries of being indifferent to human suffering and they don't deny it. Dacre accepts that "Logic and faith occupy different compartments", and is disturbed by the cool logic of the missionaries. His skepticism is reinforced for the reader by periodic excerpts from the missionaries' manual of operations, which eventually begin to mention the need to use mental control to influence highly placed leaders and suggest other ways to manipulate public opinion. Their arrival begins to look more like a conquest than a conversion.

The alien religion is clearly a substitute by the author for actual human religions, the meaningless of which is reinforced by a reference to a television set as a household god. Dacre even notes at one time that the mindless piety of the alien is so similar to human religion that he cannot tell the difference. Instead of bringing people together, it clearly drives them apart. Wordsworth and his wife are no longer really communicating, and when Dacre tries to talk frankly about the subject he is rebuffed and the two men cease talking almost entirely.

The older man then decides to go to London, without his family, to try to intercede for the imprisoned missionaries. Wilcox is hospitalized and cut off from them all. Even the four missionaries, now in custody, are kept separate from one another, although physical separation may or may not limit their capacity to communicate. Dacre and Janey have not spoken since the night they were abducted, and when they encounter one another by chance, she is hostile and distant. The early converts have already become outcasts, are even suspected of witchcraft.

Mrs. Wordsworth, however, unconverts, in fact becomes a rabid opponent of Ustiliath, but she is clearly out of her mind, suffering from paranoia and hallucinations. She is determined to kill the missionaries, destroy their new religion, and exhorts the local vicar to help. The corruption inherent in all religions is illustrated by the ease with which he agrees to be part of an assassination plot, although he insists on avoiding actually talking about what they are planning.

Paradoxically, the missionaries – about whom the reader will have developed even deeper suspicions – are opposed most effectively by the insanity of Mrs. Wordsworth and the lies she has propagated. They are also split among themselves, suggesting that their mission is not going as planned, that they have become more of a fad than a movement. Upon their release, they return to the Wordsworth's farm, ostensibly to rest and regroup, unaware that rumors have been spreading that they raped Janey during their first encounter and that they are entering an almost entirely hostile community. The divided missionaries finally let down their guard, admitting that there is a political element to their efforts, that it is possible that their superiors might wish to acquire the Earth for their own purposes. Completing the paradox, the missionaries are burned to death by an angry mob and Dacre goes to Wilcox to see if some of his father's losses can be recouped, only to accept a job as treasurer of the new religious movement, despite his lack of belief. We are told thereby that all religions are just tools of commerce and politics, regardless of whether or not they contain elements of actual truth.

The Continuous Katherine Mortenhoe (1974, aka *The Unsleeping Eye*) is set in a future in which fatal diseases are almost unknown. The title character contracts one, however, which is caused by too much information in her brain interacting with a physical problem, physiologically nonsensical but true to the theme of the novel. The narrator is a man who has been surgically implanted with a movie camera in place of one eye so that he can act as an invasive journalist, following her continuously through the last few weeks of her life. The basic story line clearly establishes the inhumanity of the existing system and the further dehumanization caused by media exploitation, but Compton surrounds the obvious with less overt signs.

For example, when the doctor is explaining her situation to Mortenhoe, he addresses the wall rather than the woman. The narrator, watching secretly through a one way glass, glances into a camera/mirror effect and cannot find himself in the image even though he is within range. This is later reprised when Mortenhoe looks into a mirror and decides that the reflection is not of herself. Her profession is to copy edit popular novels which are churned out by computer programs, similar to those in Fritz Leiber's more openly satirical *The Silver Eggheads*. Mortenhoe accepts the lack of human feelings in the world even before she learns of her illness. "Opinions and decisions – matters of faith even – were likewise a matter of chemistry."

Compton's depiction of her initial reaction to the news is convincing. Mortenhoe returns to her job and decides to continue as long as possible, reassured partially by a sense of familiarity. She also fantasizes about other things she could be doing, the novel she always meant to write, even flirts with a man using a false name. She becomes acutely aware of things in her environment, things she has never actually looked at before.

She is also infuriated because the medical center leaked the information to the media. Journalists hound her, someone told her husband before she could do so, and there is a letter waiting for suggesting that she sell her life – or rather death – story. The protagonist, Roddie, is clandestinely watching her although he cannot act officially until she signs a contract. He is in fact impressed with her self possession and determination not to share her grief. Despite his profession, however, he has trouble with human connections himself, which is illustrated by an ill conceived visit to his ex-wife. His doctor points out that he was an ideal candidate for the prosthesis because rather than feeling alienated from other people, Roddie has always felt alienated from himself, and now he has a good reason to feel that way.

Society as a whole is divorced from its own human nature. The fascination with Mortenhoe results from a dearth of deep emotion in the populace as a whole. When she and her husband visit a tourist attraction, we are told that everything is carefully labeled defining its nature, including all of the people who work there. The employees then are simply assets, parts of the landscape rather than individuals. There is also a disparity in how they respond to her illness. When people see her on television, they feel compassionate because even though they are vicariously experiencing her final days, the television makes the experience safe and unreal. When they encounter her in real life, and note her infirmity and distress, they are hostile because they see in her their own frailty and wish to reject it.

Like most of Compton's settings, this is a dreary, unhappy world. There are constant mass protests against one thing or another, marriages are short term arrangements subject to renewal and with little continuity, literature is debased, the media is even worse, and the elderly are drugged into a state resembling happiness. Those who don't care for the shape of society drop out and become Fringies, living in derelict buildings. The propensity for violence is not well hidden. Roddie kills at least one person when he tries to drive through a protest, and he is beaten by the police rather than the protestors during his subsequent rescue from the mob.

Determined to outsmart the media, Mortenhoe signs a contract to allow them to film her final days, deposits the money in her husband's account, then disguises herself in order to blend into the underclass. Unfortunately, she is unaware of the fact that her husband planted a tracer in her purse. Roddie, whom she has never seen, then disguises himself similarly so that he can approach her as a friend rather than a cameraman. As he continues the charade, he begins to genuinely sympathize with her, so much so that he eventually destroys his camera system, rendering himself blind, rather than show any more. The additional irony is that the author has just revealed that she is not actually fatally ill at all, that this was all a fraud perpetrated by her doctor and the television producer, although Roddie is not aware of this.

Ultimately, she dies because she is convinced that she will do so, and perhaps in part because she sees death as a refuge, a way of escaping from a drab and largely insupportable life. Roddie is, despite his blindness, redeemed by her actions, finally recovering that part of himself that resonates with the rest of humanity, a discovery that even promises to reunite him with his former wife and his son. Although Compton describes a dismal, depressing future, the novel ends on a qualified upbeat note, because the possibility that humanity can rise from the moral ashes is clearly demonstrated.

A Usual Lunacy (1978) is also set in a dismal, repressive future. The government and civil authorities are intolerant of dissent and abusive, the population is sexually repressed, crime is rampant, and things in general are looking bad. The Scholes Virus is a complex infection which causes people who have compatible strains and who are at the proper stage of infection to suddenly become sexually obsessed with one another. We learn about this during the trial of two people who recently went through the process, although the male half – Giles Cranston – was apparently deliberately affected by a mysterious organization known to him only as Them.

The viral infection has resulted in legal and ethical problems because despite its obvious awkward consequences, it also imbues those infected with a strengthened resistance to all other diseases. There i a plot to get a stewardess infatuated with a man who can then manipulate her, smuggle a weapon aboard an airplane, and hijack it in order to force the government to release a political prisoner. He is supposed to be exonerated when the rebels take over, which they do, except that they find him guilty and execute him instead. *A Usual Lunacy* does not measure up to Compton's normal standards. Although the prose is as excellent as always, the novel feels like it should have been much shorter. There is, for example, entirely too much irrelevant detail about the female protagonist's job – she works as a stewardess or attendant for an airline that only carries passengers who have been anaesthetized first. The satire is limited and repetitive, the characters are too exaggerated to engage the reader, and there really isn't much plot development.

Windows (1979) is the sequel to *The Continuous Katherine Mortenhoe*. The story picks up right where the previous one ended, with Mortenhoe dead and Roddie blind. There is an immediate new conflict. Roddie's ex-wife wants to take him home and care for him now that he has "come back" from the inhumane world of the media. His boss, Vincent, prefers that he be declared insane so that his own superiors won't hold him responsible for the failure of an expensive experiment. He suggests that Roddie play along with that since otherwise he might be sued for the cost of the equipment he destroyed by letting the cameras in his eyes burn themselves out.

The sequel is far inferior to its predecessor and the least interesting of all of Compton's SF. The first half of the novel consists primarily of Roddie feeling sorry for himself and making things difficult for his ex-wife and son. At the same time, they all discover that they are not free of media and outside interest, which becomes increasingly importunate until they finally decide to accept an invitation to stay in Italy with a reclusive writer who is also horrified by the nature of modern news entertainment. The invitation turns out to be a diversion. His host actually wants to use the death of Roddie and his family to make a political statement. Although there's a relatively upbeat ending – they all survive and Roddie decides to accept surgery to restore his vision – there is a sense that they have still collectively sold out their integrity. Or perhaps it is just that none of the characters have any integrity to hang onto in the first place.

Ascendancies (1980) is set in still another depressing future. The global energy crisis has been averted only because of the regular fall of Moondrift, an alien substance which turns out to be the perfect, clean burning fuel source, which falls from the sky at regular intervals. It also deteriorates into a wonderful fertilizer so that barren parts of the Earth are fruitful again. The agency is, of course, an alien race, and there is a price to be paid. Certain humans disappear after each new gift of Moondrift, and no one knows where they have gone. The disappearances coincide with the Singing, a combination of auditory and olfactory stimuli confined to relatively small areas selected apparently at random.

We are introduced to this world through the eyes of Richard Wallingford, a claims adjustor for an insurance company. Since disappeared people are not legally dead, some survivors have substituted bodies in order to receive insurance settlements. He discovers fraud in his current case, but agrees to conceal his discovery in return for a large payoff. The quasi-widow, Caroline Trenchard, tells him that the body and supporting materials were supplied by a mysterious organization which claims to be doing so for philanthropic reasons rather than to make a profit, which strikes him as suspicious. Wallingford will subsequently discover that they are in fact murdering people and stealing their bodies in order to substitute them for others.

Trenchard is promptly blackmailed by Irene, who claims to have been reconstituted after having disappeared, a process she blames on radio waves. Wallingford decides to pretend to agree, then follow her and investigate, but she sees through his ruse. Her apartment contains large amounts of cash, suggesting this isn't her first foray into blackmail. Trenchard attempts to get in touch with the so-called philanthropists, and receives a vaguely threatening call back. She and Wallingford have fallen into a quasi-romantic relationship despite their antipathy toward one another and they, and the people around them, are caught up in the game they call Ascendancies, which is a subtle way of gaining prestige and power in social situations. The problem with the game is that no one really knows the rules. "…if we could only discover them we'd be all right."

More connections emerge. Irene was released from the hospital into the custody of Mr. Fitzhenry, who was the man who threatened Trenchard on the phone and who has also been investigating Wallingford. At his request, Irene is committed again, apparently removing the blackmail threat, although we still don't know how she acquired knowledge of what was really happening. Meanwhile Rose-Ann, who lives with Wallingford although they seem to be diffident lovers at best, goes to see Trenchard. Her suspicions are justified when Wallingford and Trenchard, more through momentum than intent, agree to take a job in the country jointly managing a pheasant farm.

Eventually their liaison collapses because neither of them has played by the rules. In fact, neither of them even understands the rules. Trenchard realizes that she is trapped in an unhappy life without friends, if she even survives Fitzhenry's attentions, while Wallingford has quit his job and then tears up the check with the money he extorted. The novel is an examination of complex human feelings, and the distances we artificially erect among ourselves.

There was quite a gap before the appearance of *Scudder's Game* (1988). In 2039, the world is a more peaceful place thanks to Cordwainer Hardware International, which somehow engineered an almost perfect world with falling population, a redistribution of the wealth, and other niceties. The key to the change is a device which is a foolproof contraceptive that is inextricably tied to a device which amplifies sexual pleasure. Depopulated, much of the infrastructure of the world has fallen into disuse, and business is viewed as an elaborate game.

Pete Laznett, the protagonist, is estranged from his parents, whom he believes never loved each other and tried to make up for it by smothering him with affection, which is why he hasn't visited their home in the country for seventeen years. But the last call from his mother made him curious about his father's health so he resolves to pay a visit at long last and resolve the tensions among them for once and for all. His father is the Scudder of the title. Pete finds it difficult to relate to either of his parents, and initially decides they have not changed in the seventeen years since last he saw them, although he begins to suspect that something is up by the end of the first day.

Laznett meets Grace, to whom he is attracted, but also discovers that there was a recent mysterious explosion in the area, variously attributed to the arrival of a UFO or the crash of a meteorite. He thinks it more likely that a bomb was set off for some reason, perhaps to short out nearby electronic equipment, which his father repairs for a living. That leads to the obvious suspicion that his father was responsible for the blast in order to drum up work.

Scudder (and presumably the author) believes that this peaceful, self contained world isn't as great as it thinks it is. No one actually has to work any longer, business is mostly a meaningless game, and even parenthood is comparatively rare. The new freedom is a "freedom from responsibility", and it isn't a good thing. Eventually Peter learns the truth;, his father is attempting to organize a rebellion against the status quo by sabotaging the communications systems. He does some checking and finds out the authorities are aware of it, don't consider it particularly serious, and intend to let him alone because he poses no serious threat. Nevertheless, Pete feels the necessity to act, to protect the world he thinks he holds most dear, and destroys the one which he actually loves.

Ragnarok (1991) was written in collaboration with John Gribbin. Robert Graham is a brilliant physicist and a disarmament supporter who finally decides that the situation is grave enough that he must commit an act of terrorism to frighten the world governments into taking action. To this end, he, his daughter, and a few associates arrange to have devices planted in the ocean near Iceland, then delivers an explanation of their purpose to the scientific advisers of the US and the Soviet Union – which dates the story a bit, but not seriously. We are also introduced to a professional assassin operating in Europe and an Icelandic journalist curious about the bogus research ship. This is somewhat of a departure for Compton into the realm of the contemporary thriller, perhaps in part the result of Gribbin's influence.

The plot itself is somewhat unrealistic. The conspirators want to force a partial diversion of military budgets into humanitarian areas, publicly announced, on the assumption that this will lead to enlightenment and further reductions. It is hard to believe that the characters really believe that, given the ability of governments to reverse course quickly, to say nothing of the fact that there are numerous smaller nations who would not follow suit. The threat is that a bomb has been set which will open a fault line near Iceland, mixing seawater and lava, causing an eruption that will bring a nuclear winter to the northern hemisphere, killing millions of people. The science of this seems unlikely, and in any case they have no intention of detonating the weapon even if their bluff fails. The ship and the bomb are booby trapped to prevent an attack, but one of the conspirators is actually an agent of the same people who employ the assassin and they are not as scrupulous. They intend that the bomb explode so that the Mideast and North Africa can emerge as the dominant part of the world. The agent, Kassim, sets a timer to explode the bomb and leaves the ship, and the country, just as Graham senior learns that he is a double agent. Although their safeguards make the timed explosion ineffective, the incident is followed by a fatal confrontation with disguised American soldiers and it is evident that the plan is rapidly falling apart.

What follows is fairly routine. Graham senior gets captured and tortured. The renegade tries to sell his information and gets killed. The reporter tries to find out what is going on and nearly gets dies himself. The authorities believe that Graham's daughter will not set off the bomb no matter what the provocation and decide that only one person aboard the ship will do so, which means all they have to do is kill him to eliminate the threat. Although the authors appear to have considerable sympathy for the conspirators, the impracticality of their plan is readily apparent, and the effect on innocent lives even without the explosion is sobering. Finally a military mission is underway and the authorities discover that it was not entirely a bluff after all. The ensuing destruction alters the world forever. Competently done, but with none of the distinct style and levels of meaning common to most of Compton's other work.

Nomansland (1993) involves a virus that makes it impossible to conceive a male baby. Forty years after its appearance, males have become less numerous but still cling to power. Dr. Harriet Kahn-Ryder is a female scientist who has become frustrated by the government bureaucracy which seems intent upon preventing her from publishing the results of her research – a probable cure for the virus. She worked for the government on the mistaken assumption that political chicanery would be less onerous than in the corporate equivalent. Now she is determined to publish, even in the face of threats of criminal action against her, but her determination falters when a government agent appears at her house and quite deliberately kills her cat to underline the threat. Clearly this is another of Compton's quietly oppressive governments.

The protagonist's background is filled in through flashbacks to her childhood and early life, which also provides glimpses of the public reaction to the consequences of the new virus – chiefly misogyny. In the present, however, she and her lover are determined to publish her findings despite the threat, but to do so they have to find a safe haven for her teenaged daughter Anna. Harriet is also troubled by the realization that someone among her trusted team members is actually an informer, reporting to the ministry on her activity. She is additionally aware that she is being monitored closely by the authorities to prevent her from leaving the country clandestinely.

Compton assumes that there would not be as radical a change in society as readers might expect. Congress, for example, is largely female but the only thing that has changed is "the pitch of their voices." Some women are undergoing hormone treatment to make themselves more "male" since heterosexual partners are increasingly hard to find. We are not told much about the international situation, but it appears to be little different from before the crisis began. Harriet's attempts to get around the restrictions lead her to feel considerable self doubt. Because of the absence of male children, the population is declining toward more sustainable levels and there are no active wars. It is not clear whether Compton believes this to be a temporary reaction to the crisis or a fundamental alteration of human behavior.

There is a secondary plot involving Harriet's brother Daniel, who grew up hating women because of their abusive mother and who is now part of a secret group which murders women and sabotages their clinics. Her realization that Daniel is a serial killer makes her life immensely more complicated at the worst possible time. Fortunately, his secret avocation turns out to have a perverse value during the climax, in which we discover that it wasn't a government conspiracy after all, just one bureaucrat hoping to sell the cure to a corporation. A near future thriller with some interesting observations about human society, but not nearly as inventive as his earlier novels.

Compton's last science fiction novel was *Justice City* (1994). As with his other work, this one is set in the near future. Justice City is a futuristic prison which has become even more of a closed society than are those in the contemporary world. Public opinion has swung to the right and the prisoners are drugged, kept in near total isolation, and are subjected to regular low level torture (termed "punishment") as part of their sentences. The key players include Peggy Landon, a psychiatric nurse, Alec Duncan, a police detective, Granny Porter, a kind of trustee, and Albert Beech, a convicted rapist and murderer.

Most of the characters are clearly dealing with ethical conflicts. Landon and another nurse, Jake de Carteret, are uneasy about the punishment program and work in other areas of the prison. Duncan is troubled by the brutality of the police and the lack of concern for common decency. Since he is black, he is no stranger to prejudice and bad manners, and he impulsively rescues an injured drug addict from arrest and further mistreatment. Beech becomes pivotal more by his absence than his presence, since he dies during his initial treatment, only hours after arriving at the prison. It's an obvious murder and it appears that the only possible suspects are Landon, de Carteret, Porter, and another nurse named Serote. Although it is not in his jurisdiction, Duncan is tapped to investigate what could potentially become a national scandal and embarrassment to the government. There is also the question of how Beech smuggled a good deal of cash past the initial screening, which is found in his pocket during the post mortem.

For political reasons, the authorities want Duncan to arrest Serote. They have suppressed news of the death in order to protect the reputation of Justice City lest it be thought a failing of their procedures. Certainly it appears that one of the three medical staff members must be the killer. No one seems to think of Porter, whom the reader knows worked for the dead man in years past and recognized him when he first arrived at the prison. The mystery doesn't last long, however, as we switch to Landon's viewpoint again and discover that she killed Beech, that she had also known him in the past when she was involved with illegal drug sales.

Landon makes an unconvincing argument that they are not inflicting torture. "Not torture - punishment. A better word is retribution." The difference, she asserts, is that no one gains anything from the process - no information, no pleasure. It is simply their duty and society's requirement for revenge against those who break the law. Her assertions are contradicted to a degree by her use of the term "treatment" rather than "punishment." A prison official is more candid, stating that "justice is revenge legitimized." He also points out that the crime rate was not affected by the stricter prison system; it simply appealed to the public's desire for vengeance. Through Duncan, Compton poses the question of why we continue to send more and more people to prison for longer and longer sentences when if anything it raises the crime rate by introducing minor criminals to professional ones. When he discovers that the prison's research department is working on a medically induced temporary blindness as a new solution, he is driven to assault and resigns from the police force. The ultimate irony is that the prison covers up the murder - denying justice - and Landon is allowed to resume her duties.

Compton's most recently published novels, *The Palace* (2013) and *Back of Town Blues* (1996), which is essentially a sequel to *Justice City*, are not science fiction. The first is a political thriller and the second is a straightforward crime novel.

D.G. Compton wrote romantic adventure stories under the name Frances Lynch, and it might be useful to look at two of these in some depth. *In the House of Dark Music* (1979), involves the supernatural, with a ghost and a clairvoyant, but is not properly speaking horror fiction. The story opens with the murder of a musician in London in 1856. It seems clear that he was killed by one of two German nobleman, both connected to the violin making business, but it's not obvious which one is guilty. The first was formerly an employee of the dead man, whose violin was stolen following the murder, and he is currently courting the widow. The other is more reclusive.

There are several subplots. The widow and her young daughter have moved in with her parents, and there is considerable tension there. A street urchin witnessed the murder, but his fear of any involvement with the police leads to a series of exciting chases and escapes – and at one point he even encounters the widow, though neither knows the other's identity. There are also glimpses of an elderly woman living in Germany, mother of the first German in London, who is haunted – literally – by the ghost of her daughter and who experiences visions of her son's activities during her dreams. A paid companion fears the woman but is overwhelmed by some strange mental compulsion to remain with her. Finally there is a Scotland Yard inspector determined to discover the truth about the murder. The crime remains unsolved and the widow marries one of the Germans and moves to his castle on the continent. There we are introduced to a convoluted tale of insanity, family feuds, ghostly apparitions, and eventually the solution to the original murder, but not until after the protagonist finds her life in jeopardy and her young daughter subject to the imposed will of a woman with more than human powers. A little slow in the middle but otherwise quite suspenseful.

A Dangerous Magic (1978) is less intense and more mundane. A penniless young woman in Edwardian England goes to live with a great aunt she has never met. The aunt, who is writing her memoirs, is apparently an alcoholic, but there are darker tensions within the family. When an automobile accidentally runs wild and nearly kills the visitor and one of the family members, readers might understandably conclude that someone has attempted murder. The plot develops from there in a fairly conventional manner as tensions among the various family members grow more obvious and as we come to realize that something in the older woman's past is the cause of the current problems. Eventually there is a death and more secrets to unravel, and our heroine falls in love, but comes to suspect that the man she loves might be concealing a sinister secret. This was a much less satisfying novel than the previous book, a fairly standard romantic potboiler in the style which Mary Stewart, Victoria Holt, and others did far more effectively.

Compton's science fiction is much more complex than that of most of his contemporaries. The intellectual nature of his stories – and his relentless pessimism – probably account for the fact that he remains relatively unknown in the genre, despite a substantial body of work. His later novels were not even published in the United States. *The Continuous Katherine Mortenhoe* was filmed as *Death Watch* in 1979.

ARCHITECTS OF TOMORROW

ROBERT SHECKLEY

Robert Sheckley (1928-2005) was a prolific writer of both novels and short stories, although it is probably for the latter that he will be best remembered. He had a marvelous sense of ironic humor, some of it quite dark, and several of his stories including "The Gun Without a Bang" and "A Wind Is Rising" are undeniable genre classics. Sheckley's first short story appeared in 1951 and was followed by a flood of consistently competent and frequently very good work. He was widely anthologized and published several collections during the 1960s. A handful of the stories were adapted for television and his first novel, *Immortality Inc* was the basis for the movie *Freejack*, although the similarities are slight.

Immortality Inc. first appeared in book form in an abridged version as *Immortality Delivered* in 1958. It was then serialized at full length as *Time Killers* and later retitled for the 1992 movie tie in as *Freejack*. The protagonist dies in an automobile accident only to wake up in a new body in the distant future. Blaine discovers that he has been scooped out of time as part of a major advertising campaign, which is so frenetically arranged that no one tells him much of anything about the world into which he has been brought. Then the campaign is cancelled by the company president and Blaine finds himself on the street with no money and no idea at all of how the world of 2110 works.

His adventures are often quite funny - an element absent from the film version. For example, all the laundries are run by Martians because Mars was colonized by the Chinese, who adopted the extinct Martian language. Blaine is promptly taken prisoner by criminals who wipe brains so that bodies can be used by transferring other personalities into them. While being held he discovers that there has been absolute proof of an afterlife, although not the one portrayed by any religion. It is now possible, almost routine, to communicate with people who have died. Unfortunately, it turns out that only about one person in a million makes it into the hereafter. Scientists discover a way to increase the odds favorably, but the process is so expensive that only the rich can afford it.

ARCHITECTS OF TOMORROW

The positive existence of an afterlife results in interesting legal questions. Suicide of the body is now legal because the mind and personality survive. Some people choose to commit suicide by engaging in deadly and quasi-legal hunts to the death, a job which Blaine is forced to take when he cannot find any other method of defending himself. He is also troubled by a message from the afterlife that an insane ghost is after him, as well as an encounter with a zombie - a body usurped by a disembodied personality - which also appears to be menacing him. Various problems ensue and Blaine becomes a fugitive who escapes by means of swapping minds repeatedly with other people, a device like the deadly sporting hunts which Sheckley would use again in the future. Eventually Blaine discovers the truth about himself, that he deliberately killed someone during the accident that started the whole adventure, so he gives his new body to the ghost of the murdered man and goes off into the afterlife. It's an odd novel with an even odder conclusion.

The Status Civilization (1960) was originally serialized under the title *Omega*. The protagonist awakes aboard a transport ship with no memories of his past. He is one of many prisoners being transported to the planet Omega, which is a penal colony for Earth. He is told that his name is Will Barrent and that he was found guilty of murder. The culture of Omega is designed to be a satirical mirror image of life on Earth. Social advancement comes only through the act of murder. The laws are kept secret so that people will unknowingly violate them and thus be subject to punishment. Mundane professions like running a grocery or making clothing are considered rather unsavory jobs as opposed to being an assassin, a poisoner, a thief, or some other variety of criminal.

There is a very rigid caste system which dictates what clothing and jewelry one wears and everyone is required to be deferential to higher classes. The only established religion is Satanism which strongly resembles Christianity with some of the names swapped around. All drugs are required by law to be addictive. Psychiatrists treat people who have an aversion to killing others, one of whom Barrent consults when he has an induced dream that seems to confirm that he is in fact a murderer. But different people have different memories of a very different Earth and it isn't clear if the dream reflects reality or some kind of induced delusion. Judicial procedures are conducted in secret at the Kangaroo Court. The law recognizes enforced privileges, that is, certain activities are required under penalty of death. On the other hand, the law is designed to reward those who break the law, so long as they can get away with it.

Barrent kills a higher class citizen during his first day, mostly by luck but partly by the intervention of a mysterious woman, and thus rises in the social hierarchy and inherits the dead man's poison antidote business. The woman who helped him disappears, however, and no one will even admit that she existed. In due course, Barrent is arrested for non-addiction because he refuses to take drugs regularly. After conferring with a psychic mutant, Barrent discovers that he did not in fact commit a murder on Earth and it is now a mystery why he was transported at all.

His constant flaunting of local customs then puts him further at odds with the government who choose him as one of the quarries in an annual death hunt, which is almost always fatal to all the participants. He survives the hunt and the subsequent gladiatorial games, which means that he is beyond the law and subject only to the Dark One, supposedly a manifestation of Satan. That turns out to be a ploy of a secret group who want to smuggle someone back to Earth to foment a revolution, and Barrent is their most viable candidate.

The story deteriorates during the final few chapters. Barrent manages to board the transport where he discovers that there is no crew, although the food dispensers work just fine. He also learns that the guards are not allowed to return to Earth until retirement after twenty years. Upon arriving at his destination he discovers that people on Earth no longer understand the technology they use, that they are conditioned from childhood to conform with post-hypnotic suggestions and by other means. Finally he sends a message back to Omega to trigger a rebellion and the hijacking of a starship, and confronts the fact that his own inner turmoil led him to confess to a murder he didn't commit. The satirical elements are very well done. The science and some of the plotting are less successful.

Sheckley's third novel was *Journey Beyond Tomorrow* (1962, serialized in shorter form as *The Journey of Joenes*). The novel is cast in the form of various legends and accounts of the life of Joenes, who lived in the long ago 21st Century and whose journey became legendary. The documents are flawed by the passage of time, as for example the confusion between a board of trustees at a power company and the Knights of the Round Table. Joenes was raised on a small Tahitian island and didn't leave until after his parents had died and his job went away. Upon arriving in California, Joenes promptly meets Lum, a hippie type, and after partaking of drugs makes the mistake of challenging a police officer and getting himself arrested.

His subsequent adventures include an encounter with the House Un-American Activities Committee, and lampoons of churches, education, government, the legal system, business, and many other areas of modern human life. Particularly effective is the description of a policy of persecuting people who are paranoid so that they are right and therefore sane. Joenes becomes a college professor, visits a Utopian community, enters government service, survives a world war, and returns to the South Seas. The satire is farcical and toward the end a bit repetitive, but Sheckley wisely kept the novel rather short.

The Tenth Victim (1965) is a bit of an oddity. Sheckley's short story, "The Seventh Victim" was made into a movie – not a very good one – and this is a tie in complete with stills in its original edition. But the novel is not based on the screenplay, has different characters and situations as well as a completely different tone. The premise is that in the decadent future, it is legal to volunteer for the Hunt, competitions in which players alternate between being hunter and victim in a deadly game of assassination. The novel, like the movie, focuses on one of these conflicts, between a woman seeking her final kill before retirement and a man seeking to survive his own fourth match. Sheckley treats it all with dark humor – such as the plan to stage things so that the kill is made by a woman disguised as a nun in the middle of St Peter's in Rome. Ultimately the two fall in love and thwart the rules of their game.

Mindswap (1966) is another satire. The protagonist decides to visit Mars by swapping minds with a Martian. Unfortunately, the being he contracts with is a criminal who has also agreed to swap bodies with a dozen other people and since at least one of them has an earlier contract, the protagonist must find a new body to inhabit or recover his original back on Earth within six hours. Unfortunately, the only detective he can find on Mars has an unbroken record of never solving a case. He swaps into a temporary body on another planet where the two intelligent races hunt each other and claim not to know that they are preying on intelligent beings. Then he ends up in the body of another alien creature who has been marked for assassination.

All he has to do is stay alive for two weeks until the threat expires. To complicate matters further, his brain has faced so much strangeness that it begins to interpret anything new in familiar terms, so that he can no longer trust what his senses tell him. This leads to a kind of Graustarkian adventure story with a touch of romance, except that everyone involved has claws. There are a number of very funny passages but the story is a bit too long and anecdotal to be one of Sheckley's better novels.

Sheckley's next was *Dimension of Miracles* (1968), another broad satire. Tom Carmody is startled one day when a bizarre man materializes in his home claiming that Carmody has won the galactic sweepstakes. He unwisely believes that there is no obligation on his part other than to travel to the galactic center to claim his prize, but when he arrives, he is immediately taken prisoner as the result of a bureaucratic error. After finally being released, he receives his prize, then discovers that he was chosen by error and that another Carmody should have won. After a deliciously inane argument about the nature and purpose of error, he decides to keep it anyway.

At thi point he knows nothing about the nature of the prize, a small box, but the prize speaks to him and it has its own agenda. None of this makes any real sense, of course, and as in the Doctor Who series, everyone seems to speak English fluently. Since no one knows how to return him to Earth, they send Carmody to a planet populated by a single entity which created races from its own flesh to build a civilization similar to that of Earth, while worshipping itself. Sheckley frequently pokes fun at organized religion and in this case religious philosophers. Being god is "a job for a simple minded egomaniac."

The planetary intelligence tells Carmody that since the laws of predation require it, a creature exists which is attempting to hunt him down and kill him. While trying to elude his killer, he visits a planet builder, and the sequence that follows clearly anticipates Douglas Adams' Slartibartfast. While waiting for the builder to construct a machine that will take him back home, he is nearly caught by the predator, which transforms itself into the semblance of a ship from Earth complete with crew.

Sheckley satirizes the medical profession and organized religion throughout this sequence. Carmody eventually returns to Earth, except that he has been displaced as time as well as having arrived on an alternate version of his home world. After a brief interlude with talking dinosaurs, he is transported to another alternate Earth where he discusses the nature of art with a sentient but not very bright city which overprotects its citizens. Then he is transported to a world where everyone talks in advertising slogans. Ultimately he returns to Earth, but realizes that Earth is no better than any of the odd and dangerous places he has already visited. The humor is dark, the satire cutting, and the concept of the personal predator is clever.

Options (1975) is yet another spoof. Tom Mishkin's spaceship malfunctions so he sets down on an uninhabited (supposedly) world where a parts depot has been stashed. The computer in charge advises him that the necessary part is at another location which he will have to reach by surface travel, but since the planet is dangerous, he will be accompanied by a robot programmed to help protect humans from anything dangerous. Unfortunately the robot was programmed for the wrong planet. Equally unfortunately, Mishkin has ingested a drug which makes him hallucinate. They proceed to meet a number of creatures, many of them intelligent, all of whom for some reason speak English, and talk, run, or fight their way out of trouble. None of the encounters are particularly memorable and all are quite short. And the whole thing might just be the daydream of a bored but imaginative child.

Crompton Divided (1978) is a rather minor effort despite an interesting premise. Alastair Crompton became schizophrenic as a child so his personality was split into three components, two of which are housed in artificial bodies and sent off to other planets. As an adult, Crompton begins to feel incomplete and decides to go on a quest to reintegrate himself despite the advice of doctors. He is essentially without much emotion, his first splinter is libertine, and his third an amoral killer. Naturally he has a number of diverse adventures along the way, discovers that one of his alternates does not want to reintegrate and that the other has himself been split into two. There are some obvious jokes along the way, most of them farcical, and a couple of mildly interesting aliens, but like most of his other novels, this one is episodic, repetitive, and sometimes silly.

Dramocles (1983) is also a spoof. Dramocles is king of the planet Glorm, which lives in peace with its neighbor worlds until he receives a cryptic message from his younger self insisting that he must fulfill his destiny. This seems to consist of conquering his peaceful neighbors through treachery, much to the horror of their respective rulers and members of his own family. There is a cute section where some of the minor characters are aware that they are characters in a story and attempt to increase their importance to the plot, but most of the rest is just whimsical nonsense. This might have been a very nice short story but as a novel it begins to fray early on and never pulls itself back together despite a few genuinely funny moments.

Victim Prime (1987) was the first of two sequels to *The Tenth Victim*. There are some inconsistencies with the first book. North America and perhaps the world has suffered an economic and environmental collapse. Communities are largely isolated from the outside world. The Hunt is legal only on one island in the Caribbean where volunteers can participate in deadly duels which, we are told during the satiric introduction, have proven to be a relatively civilized alternative to war.

Harold is a simple but ruthless man from upstate New York who decides to travel to that island and make his fortune by killing a stranger. The story starts off fairly seriously with Harold's adventures but soon shows signs of Sheckley's penchant for broadly farcical satire. Despite the central plot, the novel is very episodic, a reflection of the author's obvious greater ease with short stories. Our hero eventually gets into the Hunt, is grandly successful, and the story just sort of peters out after that.

Hunter/Victim (1987), the third book about the Hunt, might have been Sheckley's first entirely serious novel, but after a few chapters he couldn't resist some satire. It takes place early in the development of the Hunt, while it is still illegal. The protagonist becomes embittered after terrorists kill his wife, so he is a welcome recruit for an organization which secretly hunts down criminals whom the law has been unable to touch. There is a good deal about the underground, but eventually it turns farcical. Despite some vivid action sequences, it's impossible to take any of it seriously.

Harry Harrison wrote several sequels to his *Bill, the Galactic Hero*, each in collaboration with another writer. Sheckley was co-author of *Bill, the Galactic Hero on the Planet of Bottled Brains* (1990). Unfortunately, this demonstrates none of the virtues of either writer. It's a rambling farce whose occasional attempts at satire are inane rather than biting. It opens with Bill having a new foot grown from a bud, except that it turns out to be a reptile's foot rather than a human one. Eventually he gets assigned to investigate a mystery planet, which is looking for fresh bottles into which to install disembodied brains. Naturally Bill seems like an ideal recipient. None of the books in this series are more than mildly interesting and Sheckley's contribution, whatever it might have been, did not make this one an exception.

*Minotaur Maze (*1990) is a short fantasy novel, and another spoof. This novella mixes science fiction and fantasy tropes with reckless abandon. The plot runs roughly parallel to the legend of Theseus and the Minotaur. It mixes anachronisms with futuristic concepts and exists only for its jokes, with only the faintest trace of a plot.

Bring Me the Head of Prince Charming (1991) is a collaboration with Roger Zelazny. It has a strong and more coherent plot, which is likely the influence of Zelazny. Azzie is a demon who is temporarily reassigned to Earth where he gets into trouble involving a precocious young girl who traps him and a demonic poker game, which tempts him. He is inspired to pursue his idea for an entry into a contest between Good and Evil in which he will create a new Prince Charming and his Princess, give them free will, but act behind the scenes to produce a less pleasing outcome. He receives the go ahead from the top demons to proceed, although there are certain practical matters like a shortage of castles to hamper his progress. Naturally his plans go awry and good triumphs in the end, sort of, after a series of humorous encounters. Other than a couple of sidetrips that felt like filler, this was a well organized and generally quite funny romp much less prone to slapstick than Sheckley's earlier novels.

Zelazny and Sheckley teamed up again with *If At Faust You Don't Succeed* (1993). It's a direct sequel, set a thousand years later, when good and evil have another contest. This time they are betting upon the decisions Johann Faust will make in five scenarios from different eras in time. The plan hatched by Mephistopheles goes awry early on when he propositions a burglar rather than Faust, mistaking one for the other. The burglar decides he might be able to make a fortune by playing along. Faust discovers what is going on and chases them through this world and others, determined to take his rightful place. But is this just a gigantic error or has the Archangel Michael maneuvered his opponent into a fatal error?

The Laertian Gamble (1995) is a *Star Trek: Deep Space Nine* tie-in. A woman from a little known world comes to the station intending to gamble and she hires Bashir to be her agent since her telepathic ability disqualifies her. Bashir begins to win steadily, essentially bankrupting Quark in short order. A warship from her planet arrives to enforce its own gambling rules, which are that no party can stop gambling until completely bankrupt, and since their own law also states that any resident is part owner of his or her residence, then Quark must gamble away the entire Deep Space Nine space station even if Federation law contradicts it. The commander is prepared to destroy the station if it resists.

Meanwhile there's an odd energy anomaly on the station and unpredictable disasters begin to occur inside the Federation. It is somewhat surprising that the editors allowed Sheckley to get away with this as it is obviously a spoof. There is no explanation for why Sisko doesn't call for help, or how the Laertians could get away with overriding the laws of other civilizations in the past, or why Bashir wouldn't smell a rat when he wins every bet, and there are many other plot holes. The situation grows steadily more absurd until the day is saved, by a deus ex machina, another alien with extraordinary powers. This was minor work, even for a Trek novel.

The third and final collaboration with Roger Zelazny was *A Farce to Be Reckoned With* (1995). Azzie the demon is back with a new plan. Morality plays have become all the rage in Europe so he decides to organize a rival one based on immorality. The forces of good, naturally, decide to derail his plans. Their efforts at sabotage include introducing anachronistic characters from other eras and general mayhem, and things go from bad - literally - to completely random. Azzie's final plan comes to just as ignoble an end as his previous efforts. The tone is the same as with the first two books in the series, although perhaps slightly darker, but the jokes are occasionally repetitious and this is without doubt the weakest in the trilogy, though still better than the majority of humorous fantasy.

Sheckley's next two novels were both tie-ins, *Alien Harvest* (1994) and *A Call to Arms* (1995). The first is based on the Dark Horse comics extrapolation of the Aliens movies. Earth is recovering from an infestation that almost destroyed the planet. A scientist with terminal cancer teams up with a professional thief in an effort to salvage a shipload of royal jelly taken from aliens which the latter believes is wrecked on an uncharted world. Unfortunately, there is another ship there, commanded by a ruthless killer who wants the cargo for himself. Predictable consequences follow, enlivened by the fact that the scientist has built a mechanical alien with artificial intelligence. The second book is set in the Babylon 5 universe. The Shadow War is over but the Drakh still have visions of interstellar conquest and they are secretly planning an attack on Earth itself. Several people have prophetic dreams warning them of what is coming and John Sheridan has to go into action again. Both are serious throughout, which is not Sheckley's usual style, but he does a workmanlike job.

Sheckley's last fantasy novel was *Godshome* (1999), which is one of his better efforts. It's a humorous fantasy in which a man facing financial ruin discovers a spell that takes him to the rest home of the gods, where he recruits the forgotten god Leafie to help him out. Naturally there are consequences. Leafie moves into our hero's house, and invites in a handful of friends, disreputable gods whose powers on Earth have been curtailed for centuries. This coterie of deities wants to create a new pantheon and a new religion, and they have plans for the human race as well. Pandemonium ensues until they are finally outsmarted and the status quo returns to normal. This would have been a very funny novelette, but it runs on rather too long, a common failing in Sheckley novels, and the jokes lose their punch the second and third time around.

Sheckley also wrote several novels in other genres as well. Perhaps the best known of these are the five Stephen Dain adventures, which took advantage of the fad for espionage that followed a rise in popularity of the James Bond books by Ian Fleming. The first of these was *Calibre .50* (1961). It opens with the hijacking of a shipment of what is supposed to be crated agricultural equipment. The company appoints an internal investigator named Thornton, through whose eyes we see most of the action. He gets a tip about where the stolen merchandise is being held in a warehouse and walks into an apparent trap, only to be rescued by Dain, for whom he fortunately left a note. In short order, Thornton discovers that he is a person of interest in the case as well, since someone tried to kill the person who tipped him off - an undercover agent - and he had some peripheral but totally innocent involvement with gunrunners in the past.

Dain clearly believes him innocent, but is keeping an eye on him anyway. The undercover agent, a woman from the country to which the stolen goods - actually weapons - are intended to be shipped distrusts him. There are also rival arms dealers, one of whom thinks that Thornton is behind the theft, and threatens him if he doesn't turn over the cargo. The action takes them to an island in the Caribbean for an exciting finish. This was a very effective thriller and one might wonder if Sheckley's penchant for satire might have diverted him from a more memorable and successful career writing adventure stories..

The second Stephen Dain novel was *Dead Run* (1961) and it is also excellent. The theft by Russian agents of secret NATO documents in England goes awry when a small time thief impulsively grabs the briefcase containing them and runs off. Agents from both sides try to track him down in a search that moves from England to France to Austria. Dain is more or less in charge of the American effort, although he has some minor trouble with an impatient local intelligence chief, and he is also trying to protect an American tourist who was the only witness able to identify the thief. We don't see a lot of Dain this time either. In fact, a good deal of the story is told from the point of view of the thief, who is presented as a sympathetic character down on his luck and desperate to find a way out of the trap his life has turned into. But selling secrets turns out to be a lot more difficult and dangerous than he expected. Oddly, Dain is the least developed of the characters in this short but surprisingly complex adventure story. There is also an exciting climax with a sports car battling a tank that would be great on a movie screen.

Live Gold (1962) was the next in the series. This time Dain is after a slave trader who recruits people from remote villages in North Africa for trips to Mecca, then arranges for them to be declared illegal aliens in Saudi Arabia and remanded to his custody. Since slavery was legal at the time Sheckley set this story, the deluded pilgrims are then sold to the highest bidder.

Once again we see little directly of Dain because we only know that he is one of the seven European men accompanying the latest batch across North Africa. The slaver, along with a Greek informer, is sure that one of them is Dain in disguise, but they are frustrated in their efforts to unmask him. The reader is similarly kept in the dark. When they finally strike and murder one of the men, it is not Dain at all but a South African detective following one of the remaining six, who stole diamonds and is attempting to escape retribution. There is also a rival slave trader whose enmity complicates matters further. We don't find out which one is Dain until the book is nearly done, and at least part of the climax is et offstage as well. A bit more sedate than the first two and not quite as gripping, but still a very fine thriller.

Next up was *White Death* (1963). This time Dain teams up with an Iranian with convoluted motives to track down what appears to be a drug distribution operation working out of somewhere on the Iranian/Afghan border. They join forces with a raiding party from one tribe and are able to destroy a heroine processing plant high in the mountains, but not before the latest shipment is carried off by another tribe. Dain wants to stop the shipment and determine the new delivery route, so they set out in pursuit, but after a pitched battle and other delays, they learn that they are too late to prevent the transfer to a group of Arab couriers. The chase continues over a dangerous desert and another gun battle takes place before the Arabs appear to have escaped once again. Although this one is also pretty good, it is marred by a weak ending, with Dain rather inelegantsly rescued after he falls into a trap.

The last Stephen Dain adventure was *Time Limit* (1967). This time he is doing some investigative work for a rebel group trying to decide on the timing for an attempted revolt against the Iraqi government. What should have been a quick, routine reconnaissance goes awry when he is betrayed, arrested, rescued, pursued, and eventually realizes that he doesn't know who can be trusted and who cannot. Most of the novel is an extended chase across a desert, which ultimately ends with Dain and his companions either dead or captured. Inexplicably his captors release him in time for him to deliver his message that the rebellion has been anticipated and will provide the Iraqis with an excuse to slaughter the rebels. He also figures out that the leaders of that group never meant for him to succeed, that they always knew things would go badly, but that this was the only way for them to hang onto their leadership positions. There are some other surprises, most of them similarly depressing. Another good Dain story, but unfortunately the last.

The Man in the Water (1961) is another suspense novel, but bears no other resemblance to the Dain series. Dennison is a sailor stranded on St. Thomas Island, hoping to find a crew opening on some passing vessel. His past and present include moments of rage and violence. Although he thinks of himself as a good man down on his luck, he is actually a malcontent on the verge of a major breakdown. Much of the story consists of flashbacks to Dennison's earlier adventures in Asia and the South Pacific, none of which make us like him any better.

Eventually he finds a berth with Captain James and the two of them to travel up to New York City where Dennison hopes to borrow money from his sister. James is an experienced roughneck himself but the two men seem to be compatible. Tensions rise as time passes, particularly when Dennison finds out that James has a large amount of cash with him. He fantasizes about losing the captain overboard, or perhaps even pushing him off the boat. In due course he acts but James is able to cling to the boat, moving to another spot whenever Dennison comes after him with a boathook. The second half of the book consists of their duel, and Dennison's ultimate defeat and death. The action comes too late, however, and since we don't like either man, the outcome is not emotionally satisfying.

The Game of X (1966) is another spy novel, but it was a gentle spoof rather than a serious story. William Nye agrees to pose as a courier in a trap designed to capture a foreign agent in France. The process succeeds and the agent is led to believe that Nye is actually the mysterious Agent X. This should have been the end of it, but later the spy offers to defect on condition that Agent X handle things, so Nye finds himself posing once again. This time, however, the other side has more competent agents, although they also are taken in by the illusion that he is a superspy. Nye is twice captured by the enemy and twice escapes, still without disabusing them of the notion that he is competent at his job. Complication piles upon complication and Nye considers running for his life, but never quite takes that step. In fact, he rises to the occasion and after saving the day, his handlers aren't so certain that he isn't in fact a spy who managed to fool even them. As good as the Dain novels, if not entirely plausible.

Sheckley was writing a conventional detective series at the time of his death. The three published titles were *Draconian New York* (1996), *The Alternative Detective* (1993), and *Soma Blues* (1998). The middle title is much better than the other two. Hob Draconian is an ex-hippie working - occasionally - as a private investigator living in Spain. When he discovers that he needs a large sum of money to pay off his mortgage quickly or face the loss of his home there, he goes to New York looking for a quick, profitable job, as well as a chance to finalize his divorce from the troublesome Mylar. He takes a job escorting a model to France, gets involved with a drug smuggling ring, has various adventures, and survives to come back in the second book. The second title, actually the first in the series, has an even more desperate and harassed Draconian investigating missing surfboards, the disappearance of an old friend, and another bunch of drug dealers. The third and least interesting also involves drugs, plus a hit and run accident that might have been murder. All three are competent and readable but none of them have the excitement of the Stephen Dain novels or the humor of his better science fiction.

Sheckley's first short story collection was *Untouched by Human Hands* (1954). As with the novels, most of these have humorous elements, but it is more controlled and less inclined toward slapstick and more toward sharp irony. In "The Monsters" humans land on a planet whose sluglike residents routinely kill one another and who decide that humans cannot be moral beings because they don't act similarly. "Cost of Living" is a mild satire about consumerism. "The Altar" is a cute fantasy about a man who gets curious about a supposed local cult and eventually finds himself cast as their sacrifice. "Shape" has shape changing aliens invading Earth and discovering that they are happier assuming the forms of various Earth animals, a freedom which is denied them within their own culture. It's one of the best in the collection.

"The Impacted Man" is also very good. A man finds himself caught in a strange time warp that is sensitive to his elevation above the ground. "Untouched by Human Hands" is a problem story about two stranded spacemen trying to find something to eat in an alien warehouse, but the humor is too forced. "The King's Wishes" is a minor fantasy about a genie who is stealing from a contemporary appliance store to provide luxuries for a king of doomed Atlantis. In "Warm" a man begins to perceive reality as a single, formless series of patterns rather than a physical location. "The Demons" is another minor fantasy about a human conjured by a demon. "Specialist" concerns a starship composed of specialized aliens who need to replace one member of their crew with an Earthman. There's no real point to the ending.

"The Seventh Victim" was the basis of the movie and later novel, *The Tenth Victim*. The short is better than either of the longer forms. The last two, "Ritual" and "Beside Still Waters" are very minor, one about aliens welcoming human visitors with an elaborate ritual and the other about an old man and his robot companion aging and dying on a converted planetoid. Although lightweight overall, it was a nice selection of Sheckley's short fiction.

Citizen in Space (1955) is a very similar collection. It opens with "The Mountain Without a Name". Rapacious humans are about to ruthlessly exploit a new world when a series of accidents interferes disastrously, at the end of which we discover that all human occupied planets are undergoing similar crises because the universe has gotten tired of our thoughtlessness. "The Accountant" is about a child who refuses to be a wizard because he wants to be an accountant. "Hunting Problem" is rather clever. A shape changing alien child stalks three human explorers in order to get a pelt, and ends up with one of their jumpsuits. "A Thief in Time" is another cute but nonsensical story about a man chased through time because of crimes he hasn't yet committed.

"The Luckiest Man in the World" is a vignette about a man rhapsodizing about the marvels of technology, gradually revealing that he is the last man left alive after an apocalypse. "Hands Off" is an effective story about human criminals trying to steal an alien starship and running into technical problems. You have to be careful what you wish for in "Something for Nothing." A machine from the future gives a present day man everything he wants, but then presents the bill. In "A Ticket for Tranai" a naive Earthman moves to a planet rumored to be Utopian, only to discover that robbery is legal - hence no crime, married women are kept in suspended animation most of the time, and other things that discourage him from staying.

ARCHITECTS OF TOMORROW

In "The Battle" humans use robots to combat the forces of Satan and when they win, God elevates the robots to Heaven instead of the human race. A peaceful human colony out of contact with the rest of humanity forgets how to commit violence or crime in the implausible "Skulking Permit." The title story is a very minor satire on Cold war mentalities. "Ask a Foolish Question" is about the ultimate computer which has answers to every question, but cannot be useful because no one knows how to ask the right questions. Not quite as good as the first collection but a close second.

Sheckley moved from Ballantine to Bantam for his next few collections, starting with *Pilgrimage to Earth* (1957). The title story is a rather minor piece about a colonist who travels back to Earth which he believes to be the only place where true love can be found, only to discover that love is an artificial construct. "All the Things You Are" is a first contact story that suggests that humans are going to be inadvertently offensive no matter how careful they are. "Trap" is an implausible story about an alien who uses a matter transmitter to dispose of his wife. In "The Body" a scientist's mind is transplanted into a dog's body, but there is almost no plot.

"Early Model" is a very good story and one of several in which Sheckley suggests that advanced technology isn't always a blessing. In this one, a space explorer is wearing a protective suit which he cannot take off during a field test on an alien world whose residents decide that he is a demon. The suit does indeed protect him from physical attack, but some of the side effects might kill him just as efficiently. "Disposal Service" is a non-fantastic story about a man who turns down a professional murder service only to find that his wife employed them. "Human Man's Burden" is a silly and rather chauvinistic story about a planetoid farmer who gets an unexpected mail order bride. "Fear in the Night" is a mild little suspense story about an angry husband who causes his wife to have bad dreams. "Bad Medicine" involves a psychopath who submits to robotic therapy, but the machine is set for a Martian mind.

"Protection" is one of Sheckley's best stories. A human accepts prescient warnings of danger from an invisible alien entity, unaware that this will make him potential prey for other alien entities, particularly if he lesnerizes. Unfortunately, he doesn't know what the word means so he sneezes and dies. "Earth, Air, Fire, and Water" is another story about an advanced spacesuit that doesn't work as well as expected. "Deadhead" is a rather bad story about a man who teleports to Mars. "The Academy" is a satire about conformity and the expanding definition of mental illness. "Milk Run" is an amusing variation of the space voyage where everything goes wrong with the cargo and "The Lifeboat Mutiny" returns to the theme of technology run amuck, this time a sentient lifeboat that overrides the wishes of its occupants. Despite a few good stories, this was generally inferior to his first two collections.

His next was *Store of Infinity* (1960), a much better selection. The opening story, "The Prize of Peril," is one of his best known. The protagonist participates in a live action reality show in which he is hunted through a city by a team of killers while all the action is monitored by television crews and broadcast live. This anticipated a number of other SF stories with similar themes, including most recently the Hunger Games series by Suzanne Collins. "The Humours" (aka "Join Now") is a novelette which was expanded later into *Crompton Divided*. "Triplication" is a set of three unrelated vignettes, essentially elaborate jokes.

The premise of "The Minimum Man" is that explorers of potential colony worlds should be incompetent to prove that a colony has a chance to succeed. This rather shaky core idea results in an amusing story that doesn't bear close examination of how the actual plot elements work. "If the Red Slayer" is a minor story about soldiers being revived from the dead to fight again. "The Store of the Worlds" is a nice gimmick story about a method of temporarily visiting an alternate world. "The Gun Without a Bang" is a great story about the dangers of advanced technology. A man with a disintegrator gun not only discovers that its silence means that wild animals aren't afraid of it, but also discovers that the indiscriminate destruction it wreaks is as much a danger to himself as it is to hiss enemiess. In "The Deaths of Ben Baxter" time travelers try to change the course of history in three parallel but very different worlds, only to run into problems in each case. The rationale for all of this is pretty hokey but the story is amusing nonetheless. The general quality is much higher than in his previous collections.

Notions: Unlimited (1960) is also a superior selection. "Gray Flannel Armor" is a satire of computerized dating services and the death of romance. "The Leech" is a kind of monster story. A spore from space that can consume and convert any mass or energy into its own body endangers the Earth, is lured into space, but unwisely shattered by an explosion creating billions of clones of itself. "Watchbird" is another caution against technology. Flying machines that can sense and prevent murder are supposed to eliminate violent crime, but their definition of murder expands to include any taking of another life, even swatting a fly.

"A Wind Is Rising" is a classic of the genre. Two men stationed on a windblown planet discover that hurricane force winds are just a light breeze there, and when the real storm season begins, they are almost certainly doomed. "Morning After" is about a man who thinks he's having a drug induced hallucination but he has actually been transported to Venus and set down in a jungle. This is probably the weakest story in the book. "The Native Problem" is another amusing but implausible story about a lone earthman on a remote planet who cannot convince a group of colonists that he is not a native.

"Feeding Time" is a very short fantasy about a man who realizes that since he is a virgin, he is the proper food for a gryphon. Space explorers find a depopulated planet in "Paradise II" and run into trouble with an automated space station that uses them as a matrix for food production. A plan to defraud a time travel insurance company goes awry in Double Indemnity." "Holdout" is a minor piece about racism in the distant future. In "Dawn Invader" a human mentally invades an alien's body, only to discover that he is not the first to do so. "The Language of Love" refers to a precise formulation of emotions which unfortunately makes human emotions seem trite in comparison.

Shards of Space (1962) opens with "Prospector's Special." A prospector in the desert of Venus refuses to turn back even when he runs out of water, overcomes various problems, strikes it rich, but has to thwart a bureaucracy in order to survive. "The Girls and Nugent Miller" is a rather depressing post apocalyptic story in which a lone male survivor casts aside his pacifism when he encounters some uncooperative female survivors. "Meeting of the Minds" pits a handful of men on an island against an alien creature that can control the minds of all living things. This was the best story in the book.

"Potential" is a completely implausible story about a man who stores four billion human personalities in his mind when the sun is about to go nova. "Fool's Mate" is much better. Two rival space fleets refuse to engage because their computers tell them that whoever attacks will lose, until one man turns off the computers and launches a random attack that completely perplexes the enemy. "Subsistence Level" is a mildly amusing satire about a future in which the concept of a rough life has changed dramatically. "The Slow Season" is a very minor vignette about a tailor who takes a job involving the supernatural. "Alone at Last" is another gimmick story about a man seeking complete privacy.

Multiple discoverers of immortality are imprisoned by a secret cabal in "Forever", another minor piece. "The Sweeper of Loray" is an implausible spoof of racism and alien biology. "The Special Exhibit" is non-fantastic, a murder plot involving a museum exhibit. This collection seems to have been drawn from Sheckley's 1950s work not selected for the earlier anthologies and it consists primarily of his less memorable work.

Next came *The People Trap* (1968), which was also drawn largely from stories published during the 1950s. The title story involves an overpopulated future and a dangerous race through an anarchistic Manhattan to claim title to an entire acre of land. "The Victim from Space" is a first contact story with an alien race that believes a painful, lingering death is the greatest thing one can achieve. A human space explorer is outwitted by aliens who invent a language on the fly in "Shall We Have a Little Talk?" There are more space travelers in "Restricted Area", this time on an enigmatic planet which turns out to be a windup toy - literally. "The Odor of Thought" presents an interesting puzzle about a man stranded on a planet where the local wildlife hunts telepathically.

"The Necessary Thing" is a clever problem story involving AAA Interplanetary Decontamination service about a machine that will create anything you want, but only once for each object. The same characters buy an alien machine that produces a worthless stream of material and which they can't turn off in "The Laxian Key". "Redfern's Labyrinth" is a non-fantastic vignette about a man who may or may not have been hoaxed. "Proof of the Pudding" is a very minor last man on Earth story. Three prospectors fight and die over a cache of lost Martian technology in "The Last Weapon." "Fishing Season" is an excellent though obvious piece about humans disappearing, thanks to a fisherman from another reality. "Dreamworld" is another routine story about a man who determines that reality is mutable. "Diplomatic Immunity" involves an apparently invulnerable ambassador from an aggressive alien race. The last entry is "Ghost V," another AAA Decontamination story. Our two heroes deal with a planet whose atmosphere creates deadly monsters from the id. Overall, a pretty good collection.

Can You Feel Anything When I Do This? was published in 1971 and contains a selection of what were then Sheckley's more recent short stories, which tended to be even more satiric than his earlier work. The title story involves a self aware futuristic vacuum cleaner that falls in love with a human woman. The hero of "Cordle to Onion to Carrot" discovers the liberating feeling of being a bully rather than being bullied. "The Petrified World" is a cute piece about a man living in what we would consider a dream world who has nightmares of a reality where everything's nature is fixed. "Game: First Schematic" is a very short piece about a public gaming event that isn't entirely comprehensible. A scientist tries unsuccessfully to breed an animal which can prey on humans in the rather dark "Doctor Zombie and His Little Furry Friends." "The Cruel Equations" pits a man against a robot guardian who takes everything literally.

"The Same to You Doubled" is a not particularly clever deal with the devil story. "Starting from Scratch" is a trivial bit about worlds within worlds. "The Mnemone" is a short variation of Ray Bradbury's *Fahrenheit 451*. After an apocalypse, a few people have memorized books. "Tripout" is a rather silly bit about an alien visiting Earth. "Notes on Perception of Imaginary Differences" is a vignette about the difficulty distinguishing among people. "Down the Digestive Tract" is another story in which we think humans are hallucinating that they have different body types, but it is actually the human form that is the hallucination. "Pas de Tros of the Chef, the Waiter, and the Customer" tells a mundane story from three different perspectives. "Aspects of Langranak" is a boring but brief piece about a man on an alien planet. In "Plague Circuit" time travelers from the future sow plagues in the past to keep the population down. And finally there is "Tailpipe to Disaster", a minor tale of space soldiers bonding. All in all, a rather minor selection.

The stories in *The Wonderful Worlds of Robert Sheckley* (1979) were all drawn from earlier collections, so the next title of interest was *The Robot Who Looked Like Me* (1982). In the title story, a

ARCHITECTS OF TOMORROW

harried man in a near future world employs a humanoid robot to impersonate himself during a courtship, only to discover that the woman he is courting has also used a robot stand in. "Slaves of Time" is a convoluted time travel story about a man warned by a later version of himself that the time machine discovery will be used for evil purposes, but he invents one anyway. "Voice" is a trivial piece about a man listening to his inner voice.

"A Supplicant in Space" is an average first contact story, and "Zin Left Unguarded, the Jenghic Palace in Flames, John Westerley Dead" is a brief, minor spoof of genre science fiction. "Sneak Previews" is better, a very short tale about efforts to use computers to predict the outcome of marriages. "Welcome to the Standard Nightmare" is also a first contact story. A peaceful race recognizes the aggressiveness of humans so it appoints a human as supreme leader, and he promptly sets out to conquer Earth. "End City" is another semi-surrealistic vignette.

"The Never-Ending Western Movie" is the best in the collection. A perpetual western is enacted in the desert, with real bullets and real deaths. In "What is Life?" a man hears a mysterious voice asking that question and discovers he is helping with a cosmic crossword puzzle. "I See a Man Sitting on a Chair and the Chair Is Biting His Leg", a collaboration with Harlan Ellison, is also quite good. After the next war, humans are dependent upon a mutated ocean goo as their primary source of food. A harvester is infected by the goo and becomes irresistible to women, and then to inanimate objects. A bit silly but cute. "Is That What People Do?" is a fantasy about magical binoculars. "Silversmith Wishes" is a variation of the three wishes fairy tale. Despite a few good stories, this was a pretty weak book.

In 1991, Pulphouse published the five volume *The Collected Short Fiction of Robert Sheckley*, but with the exception of volume five, the stories were all drawn from previous collections and dozens of other short stories remained, and remain today, uncollected. About half of the stories in the fifth volume are not mentioned above. The first of the new titles is "Meanwhile Back at the Bromide", which actually consists of three short spoofs of trite story plots. "Five Minutes Early" is a vignette of a man whose soul is harvested five minutes early. A woman uses a man's obsession with the occult to win his favor in "Miss Mouse and the Fourth

Dimension." "The Helping Hand" is a vignette in which a woman murders her husband before he can kill himself.

Most of the stories in this volume are in fact very short spoofs of various subjects, the end of the world in "The Last Days of (Parallel?) Earth," sexual repression in "The Future Lost," homicidal children in "The Swamp," participatory television in "The Life of Anyone", and marriage counseling in " Goodbye Forever to Mr. Pain." "The Shaggy Average American Man Story" stands out a bit. A man who is the perfect statistical average discovers that he is the standard by which many women want to gauge their sexual satisfaction. "Shootout in the Toyshop" is an odd little story about advanced toys that come to life. "The Universal Karmic Clearing House" suggests that luck might be bankable currency.

"Sarkanger" brings back AAA Decontamination, but it's a rather inane one about a planet exterminating troublesome life forms. "At the Conference of the Birds" is even sillier; humans open communications with birds with unexpected consequences. A man unwisely makes love to an alien in "Love Song from the Stars." Humans learn the downside of appealing to the gods in "Divine Intervention" and "The Destruction of Atlantis" is a minor parable about the effects of anomalous events at crucial moments. "The Eye of Reality" is a pointless vignette. "There Will Be No War After This One" is an overly long satire on the innate shortcomings of fascism and other right wing passions. "Wormworld" is told from the point of view of a telepathic intelligent worm living inside a planet with no conception of an external reality. "Robotvendor Rex" is another story about a human trying to get a robot to act outside its programming. The last two stories, "Message from Hell" and "Dial a Death" are minor pieces about life after death.

Dimensions of Sheckley and *The Masque of Manana* are both omnibus collections so the next book of note is *Uncanny Tales* (2003). "A Trick Worth Two of That" is as close as Sheckley got to real horror, a traveler in Transylvania who is possessed by the atmosphere of the place. "Mind Slaves of Manituri" is a gentle spoof of B movies, an asteroid is terraformed by enslaving the minds of others. "Pandora's Box - Open With Care" presents problems on a planet where elemental spirits exist. A psychologist is given the gift of communication by a demon in "The Dream of Misunderstanding."

Another man can create inanimate objects through magic in "Magic, Maples, and Maryanne."

"The New Horla" suggests that the creature from the famous de Maupassant story might have been benevolent. "The City of the Dead" deals with out of body experiences and goes on far too long. "The Quijote Robot" is an amusing but slight retelling of part of the Cervantes classic in a fantasy setting. The "Emissary from a Green and Yellow World" comes to warn Earth that the sun is about to explode, and discovers that humans are the only intelligent but irrational race in the universe. "Deep Blue Sleep" mixes virtual reality within dream worlds. In "The Day the Aliens Came" a writer sells a story to an alien visitor, with unexpected consequences. "Dukakis and the Aliens" is an alternate history story in which President Dukakis discovers that aliens have contacted our government. Worlds exist within mirrors in "Mirror Games." "Sightseeing 2179" is a vignette about a man dying in Venice in the future. The final story, "Agamemnon's Run," is an interesting piece in which people from the future re-enact events from ancient history. Generally a weak collection though none of the stories are actually bad.

The Perfect Woman and Other Stories (published posthumously in 2011) is largely a cross collection but has a few uncollected stories as well. "Final Examination" is from *Imagination* magazine in 1952. A telepathic announcement that humanity is about to be judged eventually causes an atomic war that wipes out the human race. Not very good. "Warrior Race" also appeared in 1952, in *Galaxy*. It's a problem story about dealing with an alien race whose idea of warfare is mass suicide. "The Perfect Woman," from *Fifty Short Science Fiction Stories* edited by Isaac Asimov & Groff Conklin, is a vignette about men buying robot wives because they are more amenable. "Writing Class" is a dreadful joke story in which we discover that describing aliens is nonfiction rather than fiction. "We Are Alone" was reprinted in *Escape to Earth*, edited by Ivan Howard. It's a first contact story in which telepathic aliens flee from human explorers because of the terrors that exist in our subconscious minds. "What a Man Believes" is another minor piece about an encounter with an up to date devil. In "What Goes Up" a man is stranded on a planet ruled by statistics. Earthmen have to contend with telepathic invaders in "Hour of Battle."

There is a great deal of uncollected Sheckley short fiction, almost all of which is difficult to find and most of which is of little significance. Several stories from 1950s magazines remain unreprinted and a few of them are worth noting. "Operating Instructions" from *Astounding* is a very minor piece about the best way to treat psi powered individuals aboard a spaceship. Quite a few of Sheckley's stories from this period centered on psi powers. "Wild Talents, Inc." is a good story from *Fantastic* about the problems of dealing with a man with remote viewing ability who is interested in people's sex lives. A bureaucrat goes native on a world where everyone despises everyone else in "Conquerors' Planet" from *Fantastic Universe*. "Carrier" first appeared in *If*. In a future where almost everyone has powers like teleportation and levitation, the last disease on Earth is one that robs people of their powers. This is one of Sheckley's longest stories and it's surprising that he didn't include it in any of his collections. "The Hungry," from *Fantastic*, is a very short tale of a child who can see an invisible creature that feeds on anger.

"Time Check for Control" appeared in *Climax*, not an SF magazine. A history professor has to guard a scientist working on a defense against aliens who can seize control of human minds. It was not very good. "Spacemen in the Dark," from the same source, is considerably better. A chance meteor strike leaves the crew of a spaceship with no interior lights, and the tension builds when they discover they cannot fix it. "Off Limits Planet" in *Imagination* suggests that only bipedal intelligent races have wars. "Minority Group" (*Fantastic Universe*) satirizes the idea that we can hate other groups and still be the good guy. "Warrior's Return" (*Galaxy*) is another psi story. A man with extraordinary powers virtually wins a war singlehandedly, but is troubled by the fact that everyone wants him to perform personal miracles for them. A good story though marred by a very weak ending.

AAA Decontamination is back in "Squirrel Cage" (*Galaxy*). It's another humorous adventure this time involving a plague of invisible rats. "The Mob" (*Infinity*) is a joke story about a mob convinced that a computer is evil until they are talked out of it, and we realize they were right in the first place. AAA Decontamination returns yet again in "The Skag Castle" (*Fantastic Universe*), a minor story about a possible ghost in a building left by a long vanished race. "The

Martyr" (*Galaxy*) has a man going insane from fear even though he is immortal and invulnerable. "The Machine" (*Fantastic Universe*) deals with a machine that decides it doesn't want to be owned. In "Accept No Substitutes" (*Infinity*) a man purchasing a surrogate sex partner inadvertently ends up with one designed for an alien race.

Sheckley continued to produce short fiction throughout his career. "In a Street of Dreams" (in *The City 2000 AD*) a man moves to a new city where an artificial intelligence monitors every aspect of human life. "In a Land of Clear Colors" (*New Constellations*, 1976) is a novelette in which mixes an alien culture with Buddhist philosophy.

Only a handful of science fiction writers like Harlan Ellison, Richard Matheson, Ray Bradbury, Avram Davidson, and Robert Sheckley are remembered more for their short fiction than their novel. It is also rare for a writer who produced mostly humor and satire to become a significant name in science fiction (although the same is less true of fantasy). Robert Sheckley succeeded in both areas and while it is likely that much of his work will recede from public view, it is also probable that the best of his short fiction will be reprinted from time to time for as long as people continue to read short stories.

ROBERT MOORE WILLIAMS

Robert Moore Williams was not a superstar of science fiction and he was the least talented of the writers included in this book, but he was a steady producer of adventure stories from the late 1930s to the early 1970s, both short stories and novels, many of the latter as Ace doublebooks. Moore got his start in the pulps and among his early works was a series that was quite clearly a copy of the Tarzan novels by Edgar Rice Burroughs. He was quite prolific and had sold a couple of dozen stories by then, most of which are now nearly impossible to find. Although he wrote several novellas, he did not appear in book form until1955, after which he largely abandoned the magazines in favor of short novels. All except one, *Walk Up the Sky*, were paperback originals. His one hardcover was from Avalon and it never had a paperback edition. One of his short western stories was the basis for an episode of the television series *Sugarfoot*. His biggest asset was his ability to evoke a sense of wonder about the universe. This somehow transmuted into a form of mysticism that is obvious in his last several novels, which are considerably below his usual standards.

Jongor of Lost Land (1940) is really just a novella, and in fact most of Williams' novels are quite short. The story opens with a small expedition consisting of Ann Hunter, her guide, and another man facing a revolt of their bearers in the wilds of Australia, although it feels so much like Africa that the setting seems incongruous. The bearers attack them after a mysterious voice that shakes the very ground orders them to do so, but the threesome drive them off with the aid of a mysterious savage, Jongor, whom the third man unaccountably takes a shot at, which alienates him for a few chapters. Hunter is there because her brother disappeared exploring the wilderness in search of a rumored Lost Land and her companion is a cowardly type who seems to have deserted the missing man at a crucial moment.

Jongor, on the other hand, is the son of a couple killed by local inhabitants following a plane crash and, like Tarzan, he has grown up in the wild. His real name is in fact John Gordon. He follows the diminished party and watches as they are attacked by pterodactyls after unwisely choosing a mountain pass. Jongor, who possesses an amulet that allows him to mentally control dinosaurs, uses one of them to rescue the party from the pterodactyls. He warns them about the Muros, who apparently can send tornadoes to pursue their enemies. A disagreement arises within the party and Jongor leaves in a huff, but doesn't go far. The outsiders are captured by a race of monkey people – the Muros - from a ruined city who have airships similar to those on Barsoom.

The leader of the monkey people finds Hunter attractive, which is par for the course though biologically nonsense. She is, however, to be sacrificed to the sun god. The companion gets involved in a power struggle among the Muros and in the aftermath Hunter escapes but becomes trapped between the Muros and the pterodactyls. Jongor shows up in the nick of time and steals a crystal from the Muros that allows them to control the pterodactyls just as his amulet controls the other dinosaurs, which is all rather convenient. Jongor then reveals that he knows where Hunter's brother is, and provides no real explanation of why he didn't say anything sooner. The guide turns out to be a crazed anarchist. The story ends with the three survivors setting off for civilization. Although hardly a classic and with some relatively serious plot holes, this is a pretty good Burroughs pastiche. Williams was certainly a better writer than most of his contemporaries in the 1940s pulps. Minor glitch. Williams at this point believed that ventriloquists could literally throw their voices.

Jongor returned in, appropriately, *The Return of Jongor* (1944). The story picks up only hours after the first ends. Jongor intended to escort his two companions back to the outside world, but a message from the queen of the Arklans - whose existence has not been previously mentioned - distracts him. Ann and Alan Hunter are captured by cannibals who already have two prisoners, Morton and Schiller. Jongor rescues them all with the aid of a controlled dinosaur, then tells them that he feels obligated to help Queen Nesca resist attacks by the Muros whom Jongor routed in the first book. They all agree to go with him, but the two new characters clearly have a secret agenda.

There is a party of Muros in the area, accompanied by a centaur, the product of ancient Murian genetic technology. This time it is revealed that the Muros have a device that allows them to influence the minds of humans and they lure Ann out of the encampment and capture her. She subsequently escapes on her own, after learning that the message that started the current chain of events was a fake. The whole party ends up in the city of the Arklans, who all turn out to be centaurs, but the schemer who tried to trap Jongor has bribed the populace into overthrowing and killing their queen. Despite his best efforts, Jongor cannot save the queen, who decides that her people are doomed. The city collapses as the humans escape - minus Schiller, who was a treasure hunter and who betrayed them, and Morton, whom Schiller murdered. The presumption is that the centaur people will now die out. This is far inferior to the first story. The plot makes little sense. Why don't the Murians use the crystal on Jongor? If Jongor knew of their powers, why didn't he caution his companions? What are lions doing in Australia? How does Ann suddenly understand the Murian language?

The third and final Jongor novel was *Jongor Fights Back!* (1951) opens with our three heroes still trying to escape from Lost Land. They are promptly attacked by the Muros, except that Williams apparently forgot their name and calls them Murtos this time. Jongor escapes but Ann and Alan are captured once again. Jongor receives a glancing blow on the head during the fight which causes partial amnesia; he doesn't remember the Hunters and therefore feels no urge to rescue them. Then he encounters two American hunters camped in the area - Lost Land sure doesn't seem to be very lost. The Americans are villains searching for the Murto city and they take Jongor captive when he refuses to guide them there.

The Murtos are even stupider than usual and they really aren't an effective enemy for Jongor because they are so easily fooled. Jongor and the Hunters escape separately but both are pursued and the Hunters get separated. Williams seems also to have forgotten that the Hunters used rifles against the Murtos earlier because the monkey men are stunned when the two Americans demonstrate their use. Jongor gets his memory back, and is reunited with the girl and her brother. The bad guys of both camps are thoroughly defeated. This is the weakest of the three, does nothing to advance the story, and shows strong evidence of having been hastily written.

Williams did not confine himself to writing about Jongor during the early part of his career. One early uncollected novelette of some interest is "Planet of the Gods" (1942). An early interstellar expedition finds a habitable planet on their first stop, much to the surprise of all the scientific complement. They are immediately attacked by an alien vessel. Their engines are disabled but they fire back and destroy the other ship. Although the repairs are manageable, they cannot be completed in space so they are forced to land on the planet despite the evidence that its inhabitants are hostile. They are met by a delegation of what appears to be human beings, although they communicate telepathically. Three of the crew died during the attack and they are buried near the landing site, but the first night one of them reappears, apparently unaware of having died. Eventually they learn that this was the planet that originally colonized Earth and that the inhabitants have a technology so advanced that they are virtually gods, able to raise the dead and perform other apparent miracles. Despite some anachronisms, this is one of Williams' best early stories.

Survivors from 9000 B.C. (1941) opens with Don King, who periodically suffers mental attacks during which he remembers events from the distant past, and who occasionally feels a long dead personality supplanting his control of his own body. After encountering another man suffering from the same condition, he consults a psychiatrist who suggests that he is reincarnated from a past life. The two troubled men are drawn to board a sailing ship bound for the Azores, but the ship is attacked by a giant robot octopus directed by a mysterious vessel. They are the only survivors and are taken to a hidden island whose ruler is King's apparent twin. King realizes that he is reincarnated, but from a man who has traveled through time. The entire island, part of Atlantis, was moved forward to escape a natural disaster. The ruler, however, fears the presence of his duplicate and has him imprisoned where he is befriended by the inevitable local woman not in sympathy with the cruel tyrant. She helps them escape using a cloak of invisibility created by a caste of scientists now believed extinct and there are several battles and escapes before the evil ruler uses telepathy to control King and nearly kill them all. It's not clear why he failed to do this sooner. At the last minute, the supposedly extinct band of scientists reappear, sever the telepathic bond, and after some more fighting and a brief chase, King finally outsmarts the ruler and takes his place on the throne. The story feels almost like fantasy and the plot and writing are occasionally crude, but it is still readable.

To Watch by Night (1946) is another variation of the aliens are hidden among us. Don Reed sees a man unsuccessfully attempt to shoot a woman, after which they both vanish into thin air. He recognizes the woman as a fellow reporter named Nita Ayers with whom he is secretly in love but when he confronts her later she denies everything. Then news arrives concerning a naked man found in a field and for no discernible reason she immediately faints. She is assigned to cover the story and he insists on accompanying her, both rather implausible circumstances because the story is too minor to send one major reporter on an extended trip to cover it, let alone allow a second to go along as well.

The naked man wore only a bracelet but it is a match for one that Ayers is wearing. Reed also sees a dog run from something invisible and then die after an unseen presence stabs it through the heart. Ayers is oddly reluctant to interview the mystery man, who doesn't speak English anyway, so Reed goes to see him alone. Right after he leaves, Ayers enters the cell and the young man is found mortally wounded. Although she is arrested, Reed believes her innocent and in a weak moment she makes allusions to a hidden world, the Dark Ones, and an invisible creature that murdered the young man. Then she refuses to explain any further, insisting that it is for Reed's protection that she remains silent.

Ayers promptly disappears from her cell and after a few days only Reed is still interested. He runs an ad in the newspaper which is answered by a note from Ayers and a package containing a bracelet. He then narrowly escapes being killed by Harker, who appeared originally to be just a crackpot, but who turns out to be a powerful enemy. Fortunes go back and forth for a while and finally Reed is able to turn the tables on Harker, who is identified a an agent for an ancient intelligence, presumably the Devil, although no name is ever used and there is an attempt to rationalize everything. This was a blend of Lovecraft, Christian mythology, and superscience and despite occasional rough spots, above average for the pulps.

The Huntress of Akkan (1946) was obviously influenced by the adventure stories of Talbot Mundy. Two Americans go to Burma to find a missing friend. He turns up, babbles about a mysterious temple and a trip to Heaven, then is killed by a floating ball that burns a hole through his body. They in turn are taken prisoner and forced to pass through a kind of dimensional portal into a world where hunting is the ultimate pleasure and humans are the most desirable prey.

The newcomers find a small colony of displaced humans who are trying to puzzle out the advanced technology of their captors. They volunteer to sneak into the alien city and steal some of the floating balls, which can be directed by thought waves. Instead he confronts the local princess and within minutes has talked her into divesting herself of her technology, after which she falls tearfully into his arms. She takes him to her decadent city where he quickly talks her into outlawing hunting and organizing an effort to rebuild their civilization, but naturally there is a contingent of hunter who are unwilling to accept the changed state of affairs. The first half of this one is a fairly good adventure story but it deteriorates steadily from the point where the two of them meet and never recovers.

The Bees of Death (1949) opens with a confidence man finding an enigmatic but still functioning device that was buried ages previously by a glacier. The plot then jumps forward and introduces George Graham, a private detective who specializes in debunking fake mediums and similar schemes. He is hired by the daughter of a very rich man to find out what has recently made him so nervous and mysterious. The con man, Featherstone, allows Graham to attend a "scance" in which a translucent flying object that sounds like a giant bee kills and petrifies a small dog.

It is obvious to Graham that Featherstone himself is frightened. That night there are buzzing sounds at Graham's apartment building, so he goes into hiding. His next step is to investigate reports of a petrified cow, which leads him to Featherstone's country home, where a strange addition is being made to the main building. He and his client eventually confront Featherstone, who admits that he has become the pawn of an ancient alien brain, the drall, which uses the buzzing creatures to exert its will. They plot to destroy the drall but it is telepathic and instead turns them into virtual slaves. During a military assault against the building, the power is cut and the humans are able to incapacitate the drall, which they keep alive so that they can extract its knowledge. The end is a bit weak but not mortally.

ARCHITECTS OF TOMORROW

Beyond the Rings of Saturn (1951) must have been written on a bad day. The prose is clunky and repetitive and the plot is riddled with small holes. Crane, the protagonist, is a secret agent aboard a patrol ship whose job is to investigate reports of attacks by a strange apparition that materializes inside ships. Initially he has no idea what to expect but later we learn that there have been numerous reports describing the phenomenon accurately, which contradicts the original statement. Saturn, we discover, is a rainy planet inhabited by intelligent alligators whose violent society has been subjugated by humans, who now dictate local laws. A female spy is interviewing one of the locals when he spontaneously reveals the entire plan for rebellion, even shows her a secret military base, and reveals a previously undisplayed power of mental control. There's no explanation for why the Saturnian would reveal the secret and then abduct her.

Meanwhile, Crane's ship is disabled and he has to crash land on the planet after one of the silliest scenes in all of science fiction wherein the agent, the captain, and the executive officer all act inexplicably. Immediately after the crash, the female spy breaks free and runs toward them and they are astounded to see a human woman - which makes no sense since they are within sight of a large human base. Then we are told that the government knows about the Saturnian mental abilities because of past incidents, even though we were previously told otherwise. The male agent has a hand weapon that causes enormous explosions, but at one point he considers using it on the bridge of a spaceship! They escape from the Saturnians but Crane is immediately put in charge of a military operation against the apparitions, who are another alien race whose ship is disguised to look like an asteroid. The Saturnians have a sudden, inexplicable change of heart and help fight the mysterious aliens. This is an astonishingly bad story, not even remotely up to the author's usual modest standards.

Conquest of the Space Sea (1955) was his first appearance in book form. Jed Ambro is assigned to the large human base on Pluto which is preparing to launch robotically controlled spaceships into the void beyond the solar system. While working with one of the robot pilots, Jed spots an alien spaceship and starts to report it, but he is hypnotized telepathically and loses all memory of the encounter. Ambro is then summoned to the private dome of Konar, a mysterious, powerful, and unsavory character. For no apparent reason and without conscious volition, Ambro tries unsuccessfully to kill him. Hours later, he emerges with no memory of anything that happened during the interview.

He is then questioned by a senior technician who appears to know more than he lets on, during the course of which conversation the experimental robot apparently becomes self aware and resistant to orders it does not wish to obey. Before anything can be made of that, the mysterious ship reappears outside the dome, refuses to communicate, and is fired upon by the base's military personnel. The ship has a crew of three humanoids from a far system. They believe themselves inherently superior to humans, who think differently because of a warp in space that encompasses the solar system. One of their kind has been living secretly among humans for three centuries, but we are not told who he or she is. When their captain tries to communicate telepathically with his home world, some nearby intelligence warns him off and burns out the telepathic portion of his brain.

Williams starts to throw in one device after another during the second half. Ambro's mind is taken over by the aliens, who use him to suppress the will of other people at the base. Konar tries to control him for his own purposes. A supposedly benevolent and idiosyncratic old engineer reveals that he has a secret agenda of his own. The middle of the novel begins to feel very much like inferior A.E. van Vogt. The aliens come across as comic book villains, not very bright despite their technology, and with the emotional level of disturbed children. With the aid of the alien spy, who has gone native, the human prisoners seize control of the alien ship. The closing chapters are particularly badly written, unfortunately. It was not a propitious start for his career as a novelist.

The Chaos Fighters (1955) opens with a mildly psychic agent of the Planetary Government named Haldane observing a young woman as she shrinks down to doll size and then disappears after visiting a shop which he has been ordered to investigate. He is subsequently captured himself and wakens in a room accompanied only by his childhood friend, Pete Balkan, who is also a prisoner. They communicate by means of a personal code and the friend indicates that he has become aware of some major forces at work in the solar system, at least three organizations in a power struggle and perhaps a superhuman intelligence whose purposes are unknown. He is questioned about the girl who vanished, then rescued by his old friend, who escapes apparently with the help of the superhuman intelligence, which he calls the Random Factor.

Our hero is then sent to a high society social party which his superiors think might provide a chance to discover something about Group C. Group B, which was responsible for his capture, seems to have been eliminated as its leader is found dead from causes unknown. At the party he runs into the mysterious disappearing woman, who introduces herself as Heather. Then his hostess shrinks down and disappears, leaving her jewelry behind, although she conveniently does take her clothing. Heather unaccountably babbles about an invention that makes these disappearances possible, then pleads hysteria when she realizes she has let something slip to Haldane. This is a particularly unconvincing scene, unfortunately. Haldane pretends to be convinced but a few seconds later reveals that he saw her disappear similarly, which makes his previous action inexplicable.

Haldane is soon captured again, but this time he is the one who shrinks and he suddenly finds himself on the moon. He spends several days there in the company of a group of young people who claim to be working in a mine but who have speculative discussions about the power of the mind to shape the future. Then Heather shows up, and her motives are more suspect than ever. Hot on her heels is a gang of bad guys, who are defeated by Haldane with an assist from the local leader's mental powers. They round up the chief villain and announce that a new era in the future of humanity is to start based on several recent discoveries both technical and mental.

The story is hardly a classic. Williams uses the Balkan character to tell us what's going on behind the scenes based on his observations, but this information is actually just pulled out of thin air. The Random Factor interferes primarily to keep the plot going and is never really explained. The whole story feels heavily contrived and the author's hand is always in sight. There is also a supercomputer called J used by the Planetary Government which provides useful information in circumstances where it could not possibly have that information, but fails to provide obvious information in other instances in order not to make it too easy for the heroes. As with the previous book, this seems very derivative of

A.E. van Vogt, with various psychic powers and a plot switch every few pages. But despite its many flaws, the story has some spirit and is quite readable.

Williams' next novel was *Doomsday Eve* (1957) which takes place as a new world war is raging. Some of the soldiers on both sides report miraculous rescues and escapes at the hands of the "new people", apparently humans who can teleport to anyplace they want, manipulate equipment even when the power is off, and cure serious wounds in seconds. The government would very much like to interview one of the new people but they are elusive. Intelligence officer Kurt Zen thinks that one of the nurses working in the field may be one of them, but while he is investigating he has a momentary bout of euphoria in which he seems to have communed with a kind of racial consciousness.

He follows the nurse into a wilderness area where they are both captured by a band of army deserters. They escape when a mysterious power causes their captors to fall asleep. Zen learns that he himself is one of the new people - mutants - and he is taken to a secret underground base where they are training themselves in various ways. After a prolonged ideological argument - the leader of the new people sees no reason to help either side in the war because he views war as a form of natural selection - the base is attacked by enemy paratroopers. Echoing a scene in *The Chaos Fighters*, the people in the underground base have no arms of their own with which to resist. They are captured but eventually most are teleported out of danger.

The survivors then sabotage an enemy doomsday machine and presumably the war grinds to a stop, though we never actually see that. The new people seem strangely forgetful about their own powers until they are reminded by our hero. Not very good at all. The pervasive juvenile misogyny common to early SF is particularly pervasive in the relationship between the two main characters and the plot relies rather heavily on coincidences. Once again the van Vogtian superman dominates events. Zen isn't quite Gilbert Gosseyn but he is clearly a close relative.

The Blue Atom (1958) was bound with a collection of short stories, *The Void Beyond*. It opens with a series of disappearances and odd sightings involving a glass door that materializes apparently at random emitting a hypnotic blue light. The incidents occur in space and on planetary surfaces all through the solar system. An unofficial group of men who police things away from Earth meets to consider the problem - all male, of course, since women are considered inferior on the frontier. Williams makes this point repeatedly in his stories, although often adding in a competent, even aggressive woman to undercut the premise. In this case she's an archaeologist who tells the council that there is evidence of the existence of a now extinct Earth based race that preceded humans, conquered space, and created the ultimate weapon, which has been rediscovered and is now being tested.

Before she can finish her story, the blue glow engulfs her and she disappears into thin air. The leader of the council survives two attempts on his life by a Venusian native, whom he finally takes prisoner, but the captive subsequently disappears in another flash of blue light. Rather implausibly, no one other than the missing woman knows anything about the ancient race and her records are missing. Then the woman reappears, apparently under mental control by someone claiming to be the last scientist of the ancient race. She/he insists that his people are still alive and that a despotic ruler has been wakened from an age long sleep. The woman then reverts to her own personality and has no memory of what happened after she was taken from the conference room. An attempt to kidnap the protagonist by means of the blue light is thwarted when the woman remembers that she was given a device that neutralizes its effect. She also remembers that the other race is living in a hidden city inside Mercury, so that's where they go next.

The last few chapters go downhill rapidly. There are only two surviving members of the older race in a deserted city filled with killer apes. The scientist knows his ruler is evil but even when he has control of the blue atom, he won't sabotage the government or use it against the ruler - but he will tell the humans about its existence so that they can. None of this makes the slightest bit of sense. One of the humans tries to help the evil ruler but the protagonist and his friends prevail in a not particularly exciting ending. This was the weakest of the author's Ace Double appearances.

The Void Beyond (1958) includes six shorter pieces. The title story is interesting because it presents a chauvinistic situation but resolves it in the opposite direction. Space travel is found to bring enervating nausea that cannot be alleviated. Males find it very unpleasant but females almost always die during the experience. When a woman shows up to board a flight to Pluto, the captain refuses to take her but she stows away and eventually reveals that she is a scientist testing a new anti-nausea drug, which in fact works. There's a small crisis involving a meteorite. It seemed improbable that the drug test would be set up without the captain's knowledge and on a long rather than short flight, but otherwise the story is not bad at all.

"Refuge for Tonight" is not nearly as good. The US has been depopulated by a bacteriological weapon and invaded. A few refugees find a remote bunker which they think holds nuclear weapons, but it turns out to be a faux bacteriology lab concealing the existence of a working starship. Only one person knew about the ship and he suffers from amnesia until sight of the hero, his assistant years earlier, restores his memory. Very contrived. "The Challenge" involves first contact with an enigmatic alien race which invented a device that computes all possible consequences of any action, leaving them with no sense of challenge, a deep and gnawing fatalism, and thwarted ambition. The humans introduce a variable that interferes with the calculations and the population destroys all of the calculators.

"The Weapon" is rather silly. Earth has been peaceful for centuries when an aggressive alien race shows up and demands surrender. A group of resisters know that an ultimate weapon existed which has been lost, so they go to a museum and find it in a display case! It telepathically transmits fear into its target. They build multiple copies overnight and seize control of the alien fleet. Mediocre. So is the very short "The Stubborn Men," which really has no plot. An experiment with atomic research kills one man but his brother is determined to continue. Finally there is "The Final Frontier." Williams frequently refers to outer space in these terms, or describes it as an enormous ocean, a metaphor common in the genre. The title is rather inappropriate in this case, however. A Martian astrally projects himself to rescue a human friend from some thugs. Their intended victim has invented a revolutionary new space drive, the plans of which he intends to make public, but it is never explained why he failed to do that previously to keep the thugs from following him to his secret Martian retreat. The prose in all these stories is competent and unexceptional, there are occasional flashes of colorful imagery, but the characters are flat and the plots are sometimes poorly thought out.

World of the Masterminds (1960) was also bound with a short story collection, *To the End of Time and Other Stories*. Burke Hartford has traveled to Pluto in search of a mysterious hidden race, or group of races, who manifest themselves as Martians, Venusians, or humans as needed. The primitive inhabitants of Pluto are divided into the green and blue races and they look to this mysterious organization for mediation of their conflicts. Also interested is Cyrus Holm, head of a major interplanetary corporation, whose methods for obtaining information frequently fall outside the law.

When one of the alien mediators turns up armed with a mysterious staff of power, Holm's minions try to kidnap him but - with the help of Hartford and two friends - the attempt fails. Hartford's friend Teller then explains his theory that Race X lives hidden on Pluto and has been intervening in the affairs of the other planets since prehistory, training humans like the current mediator, Einer, without revealing themselves. The female character is too naive to be plausible and inadvertently gives away their location to more of Holm's people. The threesome are captured - Einer is killed in the second attack - but it's not clear why since they don't know anything more than Holm does.

Unaccountably, since the bad guys have been listening to their conversation all along, Micki is allowed the freedom of the ship where they are taken while the two men are locked up. Eventually she rescues them - even though we have been told that action is no job for a woman - but in a sequence that doesn't work logically. Even after showing her hand by stealing the power staff, knocking out the chief henchman, and setting them free, she continues to avoid saying anything incriminating because the room is bugged. But she has already verbally committed herself in that same room.

They land on Pluto again, using Einer's staff as a guide, and encounter a couple of glowing light globes that appear to be alive. They eventually are ushered into an underground installation where they meet Einer's twin brother and see a spaceship obviously not intended for human operation. Williams gets somewhat confused here because he rhapsodizes that this means that humans are not the only intelligent beings in the universe. Apparently he has forgotten that his story includes intelligent Martians, Venusians, Plutonians, and Jovians. The villains show up and once again Williams treats us to a scene where men with guns massacre a hidden colony of unarmed pacifists. Hartford sneaks out, recruits a small army of blue Plutonians, arms them all with modern weapons - one wonders why he would have such a large arsenal aboard his small spaceship - and routs the enemy. Race X, the glowing balls of light, explain that humanity is now mature enough not to need guidance. This wasn't a bad story despite some lapses of logic, but the villains are too over the top and there are numerous plot elements that were not thought out sufficiently.

To the End of Time and Other Stories (1960) consists of five stories. The title story involves a small tribe of Venusians who secretly possess technology that allows them to exile their enemies into the distant future. "Where Tall Towers Gleam" is a kind of cryptic fantasy in which two children briefly visit a beautiful city that promptly disappears and which is probably meant as an analogy for heaven. It's not only very minor but contains several topical references that probably won't make sense to younger readers, e.g. saying someone talks like Edgar Bergen and Charlie McCarthy.

In "Homeward Bound" two men arguing about the existence of Martian spies on Earth discover that both of them are in fact Martian spies. "When the Spoilers Came" involves a group of humans who arrive at an apparently primitive Martian city to exploit the natives, only to be thwarted by hidden technology. The last minute conversion of one of the characters to the good side is not believable. "Like Alarm Bells Ringing" is the weakest story. A super-race watches over Earth and is surprised when the human race survives near extinction in war. Overall a very minor collection.

Tom Watkins is one of the survivors on *The Day They H-Bombed Los Angeles* (1961), after three hydrogen bombs are detonated in that city without warning. He waits in a shelter where he encounters an FBI agent who tells him that the area had been flooded with investigators recently, but that no one knew exactly what they were looking for. The agent speculates that it is some inhuman force and reveals that a number of agents have been found mysteriously dead or hopelessly insane. When the bombing ends, he and several others try to evacuate the city only to discover that it is ringed with American troops who fire on anyone who tries to leave without taking a physical examination for some unspecified contamination.

They return to the city and take shelter in the laboratory of Dr. Homer Smith, who has been working for the government but who does not know what the menace was. The FBI agent believes that the US military dropped the bombs. They start hearing the sound of screaming from elsewhere in the city and conclude that the bombing did not eliminate the mysterious threat - but that makes no sense since they know that there is looting and murder going on all around them. Then they learn that many of the survivors are becoming mindless zombies - yes, this is the very first zombie apocalypse novel. But after a couple of days they partially recover, and apparently women are affected differently than men. The horde of zombies is all male except that it is commanded by a woman.

Dr. Smith finds a cure for the "mad molecule", a mutated protein that becomes intelligent and takes over control of human bodies, and they are rescued by an army strike team just as they are about to be overwhelmed. There is a major plot hole that undercuts what might have been an interesting premise. If it is possible to cordon off the city after the bombs and examine everyone, why wasn't this done without dropping the bombs in the first place?

The Darkness Before Tomorrow (1962) opens with a prologue about aliens secreting monitoring the Earth, then moves to a terribly written scene in which a man finds a woman who has been run over by a vehicle. Her dying words go on for pages and read like a speech. The man, Gillian, is a secret agent who soon finds himself accompanying a strange brother and sister who tell him about a gangster armed with a weapon that causes heart failure. The sister has unreliable telepathic powers.

The story never really has a chance to jell. The sister has mentally eavesdropped on someone - human or otherwise – who is building a hand held death ray and she has a diagram made from memory. They have a friend who works for the gangster and recruit him to spy on his boss during a very unconvincing conversation. Williams does not seem to have given much thought to the flow of the plot and as a result it is nearly incoherent. The sister also has a map that belonged to her father with a mountain circled in red. Might that have something to do with the conspiracy? They assume so, despite a complete lack of anything indicating their father even knew about the alien weapons.

They fly to the mountain in a helicopter and immediately find a secret base and observe a ship made of "condensed light," whatever that means. The ship rushes past them in a split second but they are able to detect the color of the pilot's eyes and determine that he is an alien. Then they are captured by the gangster, who is after the plans, even though there is no way that he could have known about them. He tortures our hero by putting him in an almost completely silent room which, we are told, will inevitably drive him crazy. Apparently Williams never heard of deafness. Nor does soundproofing prevent sounds from originating inside the room so our hero merely has to clap his hands to hear sound.

They escape but are kidnapped by the aliens and brought back to the hidden base, which has been taken over by the gangster despite there having been no way that he could have learned of its existence. The aliens, implausibly, come from Mercury. They are stimulating human development because they need help averting a cosmic collision generations in the future. The bad guy gets thwarted. Williams forgets that characters know things and they express surprise when they learn it again. On other occasions they perceive things that they could not possibly have figured out from the evidence available. This one was probably dashed off in a hurry and never revised. The telepathy works when it is convenient for the plot and doesn't work when it is not. Williams was never a brilliant writer but this one is inexcusable.

Walk Up the Sky (1962) was Williams' only hardcover novel. Thal Parker is an Earthman on Venus - a jungle planet - who has struck up a friendship of sorts with an oversized, intelligent snake. He rushes to the rescue when a spaceship crashes near his trading post and discovers that the man he would most like to kill, Sam Helder, is among the survivors. There is also a young woman whom he doesn't know but who insists that she came to Venus specifically to find him. Parker is seriously injured and has to be restored by transfer of various life energies from the snake and the woman into his body in a particularly ridiculous sequence. Helder has come to coerce Parker into revealing the secret of an invention which supposedly cures people of various diseases, but Parker insists that the machine only works if it is stimulated mentally by Parker himself, because of an abnormality in his brain. However, the young woman says that one of his devices cured her of cancer despite his absence.

They also see an apparition of a man walking through the sky overhead and then the wrecked spaceship levitates. It turns out that there is a secret human race with advanced technology hidden on Venus and that Parker is one of them, sent to Earth to gather intelligence, where he suffered a memory loss and forgot his origin. He recovers his memory and learns that his original people are planning to attack Earth. With the aid of a renegade scientist, he thwarts the invasion and ends up with the human girl..

King of the Fourth Planet (1962) is set on Mars, whose inhabitants are assumed to be decadent by the boisterous Earthmen who have partially colonized that world. The center of their civilization is a mountain artificially carved into seven terraces. The level of civilization is higher as one ascends. John Rolf is a frustrated human who has come to the fourth level to work on his prize invention, a thought reading machine, which he hopes will cause humanity to become more open, honest, and honorable. His research is interrupted by the arrival of a contingent from a commercial organization which is known for its shady dealings. Among their pressure tactics is the presence of Rolf's grown daughter among them, who has become a kind of indentured servant. We also learn that Rolf was once president of this very company and that he resigned when he realized that he had helped create a monster.

The daughter is taken prisoner as a threat against him and Rolf uses his machine to disembody himself, but in his immaterial state, he loses interest in the physical world. He still observes, however, and sees that the Earthmen have organized an attack on the mountain, intending to steal its secrets. He also helps his daughter escape despite the risk of staying away from his body for an extended period of time. The humans launch a major attack on the mountain using savage Martians as storm troopers. Rolf and the others move toward the top level where the possibly mythical King of Mars is supposed to live, although no one seems to have ever seen him. Not surprisingly, the blind Martian beggar who appears early in the novel turns out to be the king. There is a confrontation and the king reveals his ability to control matter down to the atomic level through force of will. The bad guys are thwarted and the crisis is averted. Quite slow moving despite the melodrama.

Flight from Yesterday (1962) is rather low key. Keth Ard is unemployed in part because he has visions of a time and place that didn't exist, another life almost as real as his present one. He answers an advertisement placed by a curio shop and arrives just in time to rescue a young woman - who also has memories of a past life - from a gang of strange men and women, who seem to be possessed by other personalities and who have a heat weapon never seen before. They also begin seeing another man who appears and disappears at odd moments, never saying anything and apparently not entirely physically present. They take shelter after the initial attack with a psychiatrist, who spends much of the first half of the book speculating rather trivially about the nature of the universe and the human condition. Williams clearly doesn't understand how a psychologist would deal with his patients.

They survive another attack, this time when a building which explodes just after they leave, and go into hiding. The woman's brother had previously answered the ad, almost immediately disappeared, but left behind an ancient carved stone with which she experiments, resulting in her being trapped in a comatose state. Our hero follows her into the trance and they both find themselves in ancient Atlantis, while the doctor has to battle with the possessed minions in the present. The tyrant from the past is finally foiled by time traveling priests from his own era. Surprisingly little actually happens in this slow moving story. The mechanism by which they transcend time is clearly magic which makes this Williams' first fantasy novel. It is also another story where the protagonist can tell all sorts of detailed things about another person just by looking at their eyes.

The Star Wasps (1963) is set in a dystopian society ruled by the Super Corporation. It opens with an encounter between the hero - John Derek - and a young woman, and it is illustrative of the thinly veiled misogyny in much of the author's work. Although his female protagonists are generally quite strong, they all accept their inherent inferiority. "Perhaps freedom is not something a woman can really and truly have except in a relationship with a great man. The very nature of her sex makes real freedom difficult for her." He is about to brush her off when she reveals that she too can see the virals, sparkles of light that hover in the air and which the hero asserts can suck the life from a human being. He can see them because he spent several months training himself to see in a higher spectrum - although we are never told what led him to think that this would accomplish anything.

Since the bad virals are blue and the good ones green, they are obviously not in the invisible spectrum anyway. Derek is the leader of an informal underground movement and he is surprised to find that the man who originally discovered the virals, Joseph Cotter, has been looking for him. Cotter is on the run from the president of Super Corporation and describes his physical appearance, even though we have previously been told that no one except a few intimates has ever seen him or even knows his name. Cotter announces that he introduced the virals to Earth by essentially distilling them from starbeams - whatever those are - from their home planet, but that they were stolen by Super Corporation thugs. The executive sends his chief enforcer to the bar where Derek has his headquarters, and Derek illogically goes to some effort to disguise the fact that he's even known there despite conclusive evidence that the bad guys already know this. Nor do we ever find out why the chief villain is terrified by the plain glass ball which Derek sent him.   They meet and he tells Derek that the virals are no longer responding to their controls and sure enough they begin attacking and killing people at random. It turns out that the glass sphere generates a radiation that creates a desire for freedom, so Derek is technically responsible for their rebellion. The news services won't talk about the story because, we are told, it is in their best interest not to, but there is no explanation of why this is true. The villain insists that he has never broken the law, just used them to his advantage, and Derek agrees, but we have previously been told that he is responsible for a number of murders by means of the virals. Derek and his party steal a spaceship with ridiculous ease and head to the moon where Cotter is trying to find a solution to the alien infestation. Since we've been told that virals only live for thirty days and there is no longer anyone breeding them, they could just as easily have waited for them all to die. And army majors do not take uncorroborated orders from corporals. Cotter manages to get some green virals and the world is saved.

This was so carelessly written that the plot literally makes no sense at times. Although we are told that this future world has suppressed individual freedom and turned everyone into slaves, it appears from the background Williams provides that people are pretty much just as free as they are today. The author presents other assertions as obviously true even though they are not, doesn't explain his wonders, misunderstands physical laws, and portrays his characters as awkward stereotypes who act like self contradictory puppets. Among other things, if the world is so completely controlled, how is it that Derek and his men openly operate a spaceship to their secret base on the moon? The characters frequently gives speeches filled with nonsensical phrases like "Somewhere, in some infinity, in some frequency range, men will grow up!" There are other times when it is impossible to tell who is speaking a particular line of dialogue. This isn't as well written as the Jongor stories he turned out twenty years earlier.

The Lunar Eye (1964) opens at a gas station near an American moon project. The proprietor discovers that he is actually one of several agents from an extraterrestrial power attempting to delay the launch, but that his true memories has been suppressed. He is attacked by one of his fellow agents and befriended by another, who claims that she has been trying to break away from her boss, the assailant. She explains that he was brought to Earth as an infant from a secret civilization on the far side of the moon and given to unsuspecting human parents to raise. He was supposed to awaken to his true identity during early adolescence but didn't - and one has to wonder how he could do so if he was newborn when he arrived.

The moon people, or Tuanthans, migrated there from Earth in the distant past. She justifies their reluctance to allow human exploration by analogy to Europeans coming to America, but the comparison is bogus since the Tuanthans have a superior rather than inferior technology. He escapes and runs into his "brother", who has been missing for months and claims to have been on the moon. We then switch attention to the brother for a while as he implausibly tries to see the base commander and convince him to halt the project. Then the Russians launch a moonship, which is destroyed by unknown means before it reaches its goal. The Tuanthans aren't too brilliant, though; they give each other messages by writing encoded scripts on the walls of rest rooms. As further evidence that the Tuanthans are villains, they have "evolved" past the point where they fall in love, although the female protagonist obviously has done so. Our hero pretends to awaken to his real identity in a logically impossible sequence in which he imagines that his life on Earth was a dream, which is nonsense because he would obviously have no memories of having lived on the moon. Then he reveals that he did remember his Tuanthan heritage years earlier, which contradicts what we know of his thoughts during the early chapters of the book. The author seems to have completely forgotten the first third of the novel because he starts talking about how the protagonist chose to become an agent on Earth. In the womb perhaps?

Everything is resolved when one man runs an extraordinarily implausible bluff. Williams never does explain why the brother was abducted to the moon, or how he escaped, or how he figured out where and when the next trip from Earth was scheduled. Nor does he tell us how the protagonist, who has never heard the Tuanthan language spoken before, goes from not understanding it one day to understanding it perfectly a few days later. His misogyny also rears its head. "She is a woman. She obviously doesn't know her own mind." There is also an interlude with a telepath that has no relevance to the rest of the plot and was probably added to beef up the word count. This was his last Ace Double and next to last title for that publisher.

The Second Atlantis (1965) was the last book Williams published with Ace. It's a very short disaster novel about the Big One, the earthquake that destroys California. Following the usual pattern of such novels, it jumps from character to character for short sketches about the disaster, and many of the characters only survive for a couple of pages. Among them is a conman prophet who has some genuine psychic powers and who may be a reincarnation of someone who lived in lost Atlantis. Others include a typical family man, a vicious gangster, a spoiled playboy, and a homeless alcoholic. Most of them end up dead. There is only a whisper of a plot as the bulk of the book consists of descriptions of the destruction - the earthquake followed by fires followed by a subsidence that leaves Los Angeles underwater, interspersed with occasionally silly speeches about human destiny. The reincarnation theme contributes nothing at all to the plot except perhaps to justify the title. Despite these cavils, this was one of the author's better written works, though less imaginative.

Zanthar of the Many Worlds (1967) was the first in a series of four. John Zanthar is a brilliant physicist who disappears while standing beside a cyclotron holding a copper hammer. He materializes in a primitive world clearly in the tradition of the Mars books by Edgar Rice Burroughs, where people ride eight legged sabre toothed tigers, or their equivalent. Just after meeting some of the local humans, who think he's a god, he is attacked by humanoids riding small dinosaurs. During the battle he discovers that he has extraordinary strength and can kill the dinosaurs with one blow of his hammer. The obvious parallel to Thor is pretty obvious. Zanthar realizes then that his academic life was shallow and unfulfilled and that he only really lives when he is killing things.

Meanwhile, back on Earth, we are introduced to Fu Cong, a brilliant but twisted man who hates the world and lives in a remote Tibetan monastery reputed to be the storehouse of ancient knowledge. Zanthar is captured by his enemies while Fu Cong, who wants the secret of teleportation, kidnaps his two young assistants back on Earth. Both parts of the story quickly deteriorate. Zanthar learns to speak at least two different languages fluently within a few minutes thanks to his superior intelligence. Fu Cong, on the other hand, despite having studied all branches of knowledge from the outside world, thinks that Americans take multiple wives and does not understand common mathematical symbols.

Zanthar escapes but is recaptured by rat men and can only gain his freedom by curing the king of a mysterious disease. Fu Cong's mountain retreat sits on some kind of mystical, pseudo-scientific nexus so that natural laws aren't consistent there. The two assistants figure out what happened to Zanthar and escape Fu Cong by going through the same transference process. Zanthar leads a revolt against the rat men and their corrupt ruler. Fu Cong follows them, becomes leader of the rat men, is defeated by Zanthar, and returns to Earth. Zanthar and friends follow him and that's the end of the opening volume. It's a badly written Burroughs pastiche.

Vigilante 21st Century (1967) has the same troubling view of vigilantes that we often see today. The police are outgunned by the villains so a handful of citizens decide to take law enforcement into their own hands. Our vigilante protagonist sounds like a nutcase; he's convinced that some intelligence is directing human destiny and that he has been chosen to help steer civilization back in a positive direction by eliminating criminals extra-legally. And this is George Bright, the hero! Williams also embraced the man as killer ape theory, which has been thoroughly refuted since but which was still popular in the 1960s.

Bright survives an assassination attempt by an involuntary killer virtually enslaved by a criminal organization equipped with super weapons. The assassin, a beautiful woman of course, gives him inside information about the organization she formerly worked for while he regales her with lectures about how evil and brutal the human race is. She also says that she "forgot" to assassinate him but doesn't know why, and he says it was the force that protects humanity intervening. The mysticism at this point is so flaky that one could almost call this fantasy rather than science fiction and unfortunately it pops up frequently during the remainder of Williams' career. The bulk of the book alternates between low key battles against villains whose weaponry is essentially magic and lectures about human destiny. Although Williams had never been a particularly impressive writer, his decline following his departure from Ace books is dramatic.

Zanthar at the Edge of Never (1968) continued the battle between Zanthar and Fu Cong. Strange creatures begin appearing in fog banks from which they assemble larger creatures from time to time, biting limbs off people they encounter. In addition to the very strange opening scenes and some awkward phrasing, there are numerous grammatical errors. The various characters act totally illogically and inconsistently when confronted with the strange creatures, each of which has countless eyes scattered across its body.

Zanthar, meanwhile, is off exploring other times and worlds thanks to the invention he developed in the first book in the series, so he is not around to help at first. The dialogue is filled with nonsensical phrases like "proof is nothing but silly words walking like a drunkard in the night." The creatures are basically smaller than houseflies, but if that's the case, how can the characters tell that they have lots of eyes when looking at them from a considerable distance, in the darkness, in the fog? The novel, his longest ever, is painful to read. The creatures are eventually revealed to be intelligent aliens looking for a new home. Zanthar eventually helps them find one other than the Earth and there is a remarkably inept attempt to paint them as not being malevolent despite their earlier depredations. His old enemy Fu Cong shows up toward the end, inadvertently gets himself duplicated, and the two versions fight to the death. There is little good to say about this one.

The Bell from Infinity (1968) is only a slight improvement. It opens with a man hearing a phantom bell while visiting a bar on an asteroid. The bell's tones suggest that it comes from beyond infinity and is the instrument of some malign intelligence, although how a simple ringing could be so informative is never explained. The ringing forces him to dance and it is a contagious form of madness. It also forces the blood to rise to the surface of his body and conveys obscure information about death rites and even secret words to its victims - who are variously human, Martian, and Venusian. He dies while contacting Group Nine, a mixed race group whose job is to suppress the development of superweapons. Group Nine is in the area because of reports that a miner brought a secret cargo to the asteroid recently which they think might be a legendary five foot long diamond reported by various miners over the years.

Conveniently, they promptly find that diamond themselves - defying the odds and the laws of dynamics - so another explanation is required. The plotting is sloppy throughout. Early on we are told that no human being has ever witnessed the death dance of the Martians, but about halfway through the man who runs the asteroid colony mentions that he has seen it before. The secret cargo is another diamond, actually a device left over from a civilization destroyed when the asteroid belt was formed. A cult of Venusians is using its power which could potentially destroy all of the other planets in the Solar System.

When all transportation off the asteroid is halted, a group of miners walk out through secret passages to the opposite side - which serves no obvious purpose given that there is no food, air, or transportation there - simply so the author can use them to provide information to the good guys, who want to sneak into the colony. The space traveling Venusians don't know what electricity is. The threat is eliminated, the evil Venusians defeated, and civilization is saved from a fate most never knew threatened them. Williams recaptured some of his sense of wonder in this one, but it's still not a very good book.

ARCHITECTS OF TOMORROW

Zanthar at Moon's Madness (1968) is rather chaotic. All over the Earth, groups of people have begun spontaneously dancing after which they disappear through glass doors that materialize out of nowhere. There are also some strange spheres that fall from the sky whose nature is initially unknown. Zanthar is part of a group exploring the moon and he finds a city of mutant women who hate men. There are also people who can walk through walls and, naturally, Zanthar's nemesis Fu Cong is back to make more trouble. Williams suggests that the universe we perceive is not the real one, or at least not a complete representation of reality, and this vague blend of mysticism and quantum physics is pervasive in his late work. The moon women have mutated and live for thousands of years. Fu Cong gets thwarted and the moon women become somewhat reconciled with males. The story has a comic book feel throughout and even the villains - Fu Cong included - are really not all that villainous. Williams was to bring Zanthar's adventures to a close in his next book.

Zanthar at Trip's End (1969) was no improvement. Fu Cong has made a new discovery, a kind of mental wind that blows people out of their bodies and carries them off to some other plane of reality. Zanthar figures out what is going on and who is responsible and sets out to save the world once again. Along the way, his two assistants are captured - again - and have to fend for themselves in a strange environment until they can be rescued. The metaphysical wanderings are frequent and annoying. Despite the title, this was clearly not meant to be the final book in the series - Fu Cong escapes once more - but either Williams never completed the next or the publisher rejected it. This was also his final book for Lancer and the last few books of his career were split among three different publishers.

When Two Worlds Meet (1970) contains two previously collected stories, plus four never previously in book form, all set on Mars. The first and longest of these is "When Two Worlds Meet" and it introduces some elements that Williams later reworked in *King of the Fourth Planet*. A scientist is posing as a humble electrician in an attempt to discover the secret of Martian technology which is so powerful that Earthmen are allowed on that planet only on sufferance. A woman unwisely ventures into forbidden territory and puts his plan in jeopardy. With the aid of some rebellious slaves, he escapes with some of the technology but an otherwise good story is marred by the contrived ending in which he comes up with three new inventions to save them in a matter of a couple of days.

In "Aurochs Came Walking" a man tries to ferret out the secrets of lost Martian technology despite the animosity of a local witch doctor. "On Pain of Death" is a rather over long piece about humans trapped in a Martian artifact. "The Sound of Bugles" features a Martian race that has the ability to mentally create matter out of nothingness in whatever form they desire. It's the best story in the collection. Williams' work from the 1950s is almost always better than his later efforts.

Beachhead Planet (1970) opens with a helicopter full of tourists being shot down by an unlikely two headed alien creature lurking in an abandoned mine near a renovated ghost town. The hero is John Valthor, a scientist who is virtually a clone of Zanthar from the earlier series, which raises suspicions that this was a modified version of a rejected novel. There are even two assistants who closely resemble Zanthar's crew. They are concerned that aliens will arrive on Earth and represent themselves as benevolent while hiding a secret aggressive agenda. The aliens come from other realities rather than other planets. There is a strong theme of mysticism in this novel as well, but it is an inept, implausible, and poorly constructed story that is more talkative than adventurous and never engages the reader even remotely.

Now Comes Tomorrow (1971) is also disappointing. In the not too distant future, a new fatal disease has begun to spread. Cindy Northcott is diagnosed with it and given three months to live, although an alternate possibility is cryogenic freezing until a theoretical cure is discovered. At the same time, an indigent man has visions of a kind of superhuman force that exists within human consciousness and a scientist obsessed with avoiding death wonders if there might be a possibility of cheating it. Northcott and various others eventually are revived in a future world where humans have transcended their old forms and habits. At this point the story become nearly unintelligible. Curtis books, who published it, did not last long and I always suspected that they never even read the manuscripts they published. Williams would also send them his rambling autobiography, *Love Is Forever, We Are for Tonight*, which they also published as a science fiction novel even though it is clearly nonfiction.

Seven Tickets to Hell (1972) was part of the short lived Frankenstein Horror series, which wasn't a series and didn't involve Frankenstein. The narration goes back and forth between present tense and past tense narration, probably not purposefully but simply because Williams forgot he was trying to write in present tense. It also occasionally switches to second person narration, which is even more bewildering. The story involves a narcotics agent who stumbles into an occult mystery which encompasses ancient gods, the living dead, and giant worms tunneling through the Earth. The plot makes no sense, the writing is dreadful, and this is easily his worst book.

Sinister Paradise (2010) was the first of two posthumous collections. The first story is "The Lost Warship." It is only significant because it may be the first story in which a warship is displaced in time, antecedent of "Hawk Among the Doves" by Dean McLaughlin, the movie *The Final Countdown*, the works of Taylor Anderson, and others. A World War II battleship passes through a fault in time and ends up in prehistory, but almost immediately sights mysterious, advanced aircraft. They find a malevolent city of humans who have developed aircraft and other wonders but have yet to discover the wheel! Against expectations, they don't find the way back to the present. One of the main characters dies but the other discovers that there are two rival superhumans, brothers, and that one is good and one is evil. It turns out one of the searchers is the hidden superman, who altered his own memories, which is a clever but not plausible conclusion.

"Be It Ever Thus" is a very minor piece about a group of alien children on a tour of conquered Earth. "Thompson's Cat" is about space travelers who find a depopulated planet, then have to solve the mystery of a deadly plague. The title story takes place on a mysterious island that is only intermittently visible and which is populated by castaways from various places. The island is also home to a giant predatory bird.

Time Tolls for Toro (2014) reprints two stories from *To the End of Time*, the title story plus "When the Spoilers Came," but the rest were previously uncollected. "Time Tolls for Toro" is a rather hectic story about a gangster who kidnaps a scientist who invented the first time machine in order to escape from the police. Cause and effect are a bit confused along the way. "Find Me in Eternity" was potentially an interesting piece about a man who encounters his immortal ancestor by chance. The set up just doesn't work. The immortal is mistaken for the younger man when he is in an accident and hospitalized, but how would the hospital have known to call the younger man's wife? He wouldn't have had identification linked to her or with her address, and no matter how close the physical resemblance, she would not have been fooled once he regained consciousness. And if he's been so secretive about his longevity, why does he blurt out the whole story to the protagonist without prompting? And if he ages only one year for every thirty, why wasn't something noticed when he was a child? When the rich, elderly man visits the lab where they're studying the older man, he recognizes him as someone he knew decades earlier. But if that's the case, and since he is a frequent visitor, why didn't he previously notice that the protagonist looks exactly like him as well? Williams had clearly not thought through the consequences of his premise.

"The World of Reluctant Virgins" opens with what appears to be the first landing on the moon, but the astronauts discover an underground colony of humans who settled there in 1887, thanks to the existence of abandoned cities beneath the surface. The surprise is that the secret of longevity exists on the moon, but it also causes sterility, which poses an interesting problem.. "The Soul Makers" takes place during an apocalyptic world war. Robot brains have been developed but for some reason they cannot be compelled to kill humans. An investigation is launched when several robots go missing and eventually we discover that humanity is doomed by radiation and the robots are creating a civilization that may be able to bring humanity back to life when the radiation has died away.

"The Diamond Images" is a familiar Williams plot. Rapacious men from Earth try to loot a temple on Venus and discover the Venusians have extraordinary powers. "The Metal Martyr" is a very minor story about a robot that thinks it's a man. Two men try to track down a third with more than human powers in "Danger Is My Destiny." They believe he is behind a staged death and assume that he is hiding from some unknown enemy. A boy who could walk through walls turns out to be an alien in "The Way Out." "The Man from Space" is the weakest in the book. A cab driver is secretly helping a clandestine alien invasion, but the aliens aren't what he expects. Most of the author's better stories had been previously collected so this volume is of marginal interest.

Despite his many faults as a writer, Williams is above average for the pulp SF adventure of the 1940s and 1950s. His reputation began to slip during the 1960s as standards for publication rose and his last few novels were scarcely noticed. He did occasionally evoke an atmosphere of mystery and wonder in his stories, but he usually squandered it by making elementary plotting errors or having his characters launch into awkward speeches. He apparently became interested in mysticism late in his life and his last few novels occasionally feel more like fantasy than science fiction. It is a shame that his imaginative skills were not more disciplined.

ALAN E. NOURSE

Alan E. Nourse (1928-1992) was one of the few science fiction writers who was successful both with adult an young adult novels. *Trouble on Titan*, a young adult adventure, was his first novel. Nourse made his living as a medical doctor but supplemented it by writing. Although he is a rather minor figure in the genre, several of his stories – particularly "Brightside Crossing" – are highly regarded. His bestselling novel was the mainstream novel, *Intern* as by Doctor X, and he wrote several books of fiction and non-fiction, about the medical profession, some for younger readers. He was briefly an actor doing small parts during the early 1950s. Several of his stories and the novel *The Mercy Men* refer to the Hoffman Medical Institute, but some of the stories contradict others and it is not properly a series.

Trouble on Titan (1954) includes an introduction in which the author lauds the potential of science fiction as an outlet for unfettered imagination but points out that he felt constrained not to contradict anything that was known about Saturn and its moons. He was writing this before the existence of the moon Themis had been disproved and before Janus, the real tenth moon, was discovered, but he was already skeptical of the former's existence. The story was meant for young adults and was one of the highly regarded "Winston Juveniles" which graced many a school library.

The setting is a familiar one, and the time frame is just before 2200. Venus and Mars are being colonized but Earth still maintains control over the entire solar system. The protagonist, Tucker Benedict, has just graduated from high school and is about to be reunited with his father after the latter's three year stint on Mars. His mother died many years earlier. Borrowing from Heinlein, Nourse suggests that efficient management of solar energy would make rolling roads crossing the entire continent possible, eliminating the need for trucks or trains to carry freight. He actually underestimated how long it would take to land on the moon, pegging it at 1976 (the actual first landing was in 1969). Virtually unlimited power has made Earth a near paradise in some ways, but there are indications that not everyone thinks so. The colonies on Titan, which is where the metal is mined that is essential to the power system, are populated almost entirely by "convicts and rebels", suggesting that at least some of them are political prisoners.

Tucker's father is reassigned to Titan to try to head off a threatened rebellion and he wants his son to accompany him. Tucker initially considers the people on Titan "scum" and feels that it would be a waste of time for him to go, particularly as he has just been offered a full scholarship to a prestigious college. There is a bit of a leap of faith required from the reader here. Someone sends a letter bomb to Tucker's father. Tucker discovers it, assumes his father's life is in danger, and decides to go with him to Titan after all. But he doesn't tell his father why.

The trip to Titan is not described in any detail and when they arrive the colony is in the midst of a crisis. Factions among the colonists threaten any attempt at reconciliation with Earth. Tucker also meets David Torm, son of the colony leader, and although they do not get along at first, it is evident that they are going to end up being friends. An attempt to kill them, along with the senior Torm, is averted but in a not entirely plausible manner. Tucker senior suspects it was all a ruse to convince him of a schism in the colony that doesn't really exist. He also refuses to believe that the colonists are being systematically persecuted and deprived of supplies that could make their life more bearable, although Tucker is inclined to accept the statements made by the Torms.

The living conditions in the colony are also pretty obviously terrible, but that doesn't shake his father's skepticism either. Eventually the two boys discover the colony's secret, a rebuilt spaceship. They also learn that the ship is supposed to take the whole colony to another star system on conventional drive, which would take three centuries. The amount of food and supplies needed to support five hundred people for three hundred years would certainly bulk far more than a simple exploration ship would hold, let alone the people themselves. Of course, the villains actually plan that only a few will go, the rest doomed to die when they destroy the mining colony. News of this completely and inexplicably reverses the stance of Benedict senior and after that it's just a case of chasing down the bad guys.

There are certain inherent problems with young adult fiction that are difficult to avoid. The young hero almost always has to be instrumental in solving the main conflict in the story and this usually feels contrived to adult readers. That solution frequently results from the protagonist either being allowed to do things that aren't entirely plausible, or having him or her disobey authority figures, not always with justification. Of course, the author is in control and the outcome is preordained, but it still fails to ring true at times. The biggest problem in this particular novel is that in order for Tucker to save the day, his father - who is supposed to be an effective manager and negotiator - has to act stupidly throughout the crisis until his son helps him see the light. Unfortunately this makes the father into an obvious bigot and his reversal later just doesn't fit with his character as previously revealed.

The boys find the answer - revelation of a secret project - more by accident than design. There are also a couple of things that should make the reader scratch his head. For example, why would mines on Titan have wooden support beams? It does not make sense that the government would ship lumber aboard the infrequent supply ships. And when they find the rebuilt ship, the boys immediately conclude that it must have an interstellar drive - but how would they come to that conclusion if it is visually indistinguishable from any other Earth ship? It was a first novel and it has some very strong scenes, but it still fails to be convincing as a whole. It is also interesting that in the final battle, all of the adults have lethal weapons but the boys are limited to stun guns, a frequently imposed restriction on young adult novels that would later lead to the rejection of Heinlein's *Starship Troopers*, which had to be published as an adult novel instead.

Nourse's first adult novel was *A Man Obsessed* (1955), half of an Ace Double that was later expanded and reprinted as *The Mercy Men* (1968). Jeff Meyer has spent years trying to track down and kill Paul Conroe, whom he believes was responsible for the death of his father, and just as he gets close his quarry escapes into a mysterious medical center, rumored to contain a contingent of the Mercy Men, a proscribed medical group that carries out illegal experiments on human volunteers. Meyer pretends to be interested in volunteering himself in order to pursue Conroe. The doctor who screens him suspects his motives but conditionally approves him for the program. Inside the facility, he runs into a woman whom he thinks has a connection to Conroe, although he lacks details, but it turns out he is wrong. Instead, she has some kind of psychic ability to affect the odds in gambling games so that she wins more than she loses. But it turns out that Meyer has a similar ability and when they're in the same room, probabilities become random and the results are unpredictable. While searching for Conroe, he discovers that the doctors are actually working toward a cure for a mental disease which is slowly spreading throughout the human race, contributing to political and business collapses in some unspecified fashion.

Meyer discovers that his father, whom he barely remembers, was a doctor working on this very same project, and that his research was skewed by an unknown force, presumably a version of the same ESP that his son is now exhibiting. We then learn that his pursuit of Conroe was actually engineered to lure him to the medical center, which is so wildly implausible and impractical that it undercuts the credibility of the entire plot. And finally Meyer and the reader discover that he has an entire suite of psychic powers including psychokinesis, which all manifest themselves when they are needed. The original version is claustrophobic, slow paced, and at times confusing because there are gaps in the information we need to understand what's happening. The enlarged version corrects some but not all of these problems, provides a little more background though nothing very significant, and updates several references that became dated.

Rocket to Limbo (1957) opens with the launch of a generation starship, then skips more than three centuries into the future to follow the adventures of Lars Heldrigsson, a young scientist in a future where faster than light drive has made it possible to explore nearby stars, although no trace of the pioneering starship has ever been found. This is another young adult novel so the political background is predictably sketchy, but Earth's wild places have been settled and the population is booming, so the colonies on other worlds are considered a way of reducing the pressure, although in fact with only a handful of ships and a round trip that takes months, there is no possible way that they could be doing anything to slow population growth, let alone reverse it. Lars' parents don't understand why he can't just find new frontiers on Earth, setting up a generational conflict common to much science fiction of this era. Lars is about to go on his first star voyage on an exploratory mission but he encounters unusual security strictness at the site and the ship's officers are tight lipped about it. Even worse, and also common in young adult science fiction, he discovers that an old enemy from his college days has also been assigned to the ship, and that the ship is not going to the planet to which it is official designated. College apparently comes early since Lars is only eighteen.

Shortly after takeoff, the truth gets out. They are traveling to a distant star to find out what happened to an earlier expedition that ceased communicating after landing, and whose last broadcast suggested the possibility that there were intelligent aliens on that world, the first such aliens humans would have ever encountered. And just in case, the ship has been armed with nuclear weapons, although the rationale for this is never explained. As the journey continues, Lars discovers that his ex-classmate has a personal grudge against the captain because his father died under the man's command. He skillfully manipulates several crew members, pushing for them to commit mutiny and turn the ship around, playing on their fears although his agenda is simple revenge. There's a bit of contradiction in the set up. The captain is acting under orders from his superiors but Lars accepts that by misleading the crew he broke the law and is therefore personally liable and could be prosecuted. The two statements clearly conflict.

They reach the planet and spot the wreckage of the missing starship, as well as sight of what might be a single alien city in an otherwise deserted landscape. Since Earth received messages sent after the ship landed, and since no one could possibly have survived the crash, this poses a puzzling problem for Lars and his shipmates. The solution is that the crashed ship is not in fact the one they think it is but the generation starship launched at the beginning of the story. There is also a floating city inhabited by telepathic aliens - who look like humans - to which the crew is eventually transported. The supposed aliens are actually descendants of the colony ship's complement, and they have been trained to use telepathy, psychokinesis, and teleportation by the mysterious Masters, whom we never meet, but who are members of a galactic civilization. The story pretty much falls to pieces once they reach the city, with the two teenage characters mastering the various ESP talents in a matter of days and saving the day.

Scavengers in Space (1959), an expansion of "Gold in the Sky", follows the pattern of Nourse's young adult fiction. Two young males become friends despite some initial differences and together solve an adult problem. There are virtually no female characters in any of these novels; in all three the protagonist's mother is dead before the story begins. Tom and Greg Hunter don't believe that their father's death while exploring the asteroid belt was an accident. They are convinced that the mining corporation, Jupiter Equilateral, is responsible. But there is no evidence of their involvement, and for some reason their father ordered his partner to leave the area shortly before his fuel tank exploded. The authorities are powerless to act without something more substantial than suspicion because of a delicate balance of power between the civil government and the corporations, but the brothers are not similarly constrained. When an official from the company offers them a ridiculously high price for their father's claims, the boys smell a rat and refuse, determined to go out to the Belt and investigate for themselves, a decision reinforced when their father's partner indicates that there was in fact some kind of great discovery, although even he doesn't know what it was.

Almost as soon as they reach their mining claim, they are attacked openly by a company ship. One of the brothers and their single crewmate are captured. During the battle, a scout ship is launched and the bad guys, assuming the other brother is making a run for it, destroy it with a missile. Naturally it was a ruse. They are reunited aboard the hostile ship and that's when they realize that their father's hand weapon has been replaced by another clearly of alien manufacture. They use the weapon - a disintegrator - to escape but the company insists that they were the attackers and it looks like no one is going to do anything to help them after all.

Traps are set after the brothers realize that their father discovered remnants of an ancient civilization and the secret of interstellar drive. The chief villain is captured and the boys are heroes. The closing chapters seem rather rushed and some things fall together too neatly but otherwise it's not bad at all. There are some minor bits that are dated or illogical. Telephone booths on Mars seem very unlikely and the spaceship's log is recorded on tape. And why do the ships have major weaponry when there has been no contact with any aliens and humanity is united under a single government? Once again the two teenagers only have stun guns, consistent with the general prohibition against deadly weapons in the hands of young adults in science fiction of the 1950s.

ARCHITECTS OF TOMORROW

Star Surgeon (1960) is also theoretically for young adults although a shorter version was serialized in *Amazing*. Dal Timbar is a member of the most successful race in the galaxy. He is humanoid but not enough to pass for human when he enrolls in Earth's medical school. Humanity is a probationary member of the galactic community whose greatest asset is that they are the only race to have mastered the life sciences, and therefore are for all practical purposes the only doctors in the galaxy. This is a pretty big lump of disbelief to suspend all at once, but it's necessary to setup the conflict.

Some influential humans want Dal disqualified because they fear that if aliens can become doctors, humans will lose their advantage. Nevertheless, Dal is assigned to a three man medical patrol ship with his only human friend and another young man who seems to be under the influence of those opposed to his participation in the program. The atmosphere aboard the ship is therefore strained although initially at least their professionalism overcomes their personal animosities. Dal's race also possesses a kind of pet/symbiote, the fuzzies, with whom they are able to influence the emotions of others, although Dal considers it unethical to use this ability.

The trio travel around a bit, solve some routine problems, have some minor clashes and some minor reconciliations, enough to establish that even the hostile member isn't really a villain. Then they receive a distress call from an uncharted planet from members of an unknown race - who conveniently have been listening to interstellar broadcasts and can speak the universal language. They are suffering from a plague whose origin is unknown, and since our heroes know nothing of their physiology, they are hard pressed to find a solution. This, of course, is an instance where they should have called for more experienced help, but they fail to do so for reasons never explained. The solution, which they realize only late in the game, is that the infected creatures are not intelligent after all; it is the virus that is intelligent, and coincidentally Dal's symbiote can reproduce almost without limit and provide a better host. That revelation is followed by the final confrontation with the man chiefly responsible for Dal's problems and since we've known all along that he has heart trouble, it's no surprise that he has a heart attack and Dal has to save him. Not badly done, but there are just too many coincidences to be convincing.

ARCHITECTS OF TOMORROW

The Invaders Are Coming (1959, magazine title *Sign of the Tiger*), a collaboration with J.A. Meyer, was meant to be an adult novel. It takes place some years after a general economic collapse has led to a kind of benevolent dictatorship in the US, which dominates much of the world. The space program has been ended and the military is much in evidence. Even more powerful, however, is the Department of Internal Affairs, one of whose highest officials is Julian Bahr, a man prone to violence and not particularly fussy about obeying the law. When someone steals radioactive material from a power plant, after which it is destroyed in an explosion before it can be recovered, Bahr seizes the commander of the plant and illegally interrogates him, convinced the man was complicit in the theft, perhaps without being aware of it. We also learn that some years earlier three UFOs were sighted in various parts of the world, but that they disappeared and have been more or less forgotten. When Bahr's superior dies of a heart attack, he is temporarily in charge of the agency even though his psych profile should disqualify him for the job. Even worse, the story of the theft from the power plant leaks, and is followed almost immediately by reports that an alien spaceship has landed in Canada.

It becomes evident about half way through the novel that the aliens are a hoax designed to force the government, which has been in a rut for a generation, to choose a new path that includes a resumption of the space program. The resemblance to Agnew H. Bahnson's *The Stars Are Too High*, also published in 1959, is surprisingly strong. As the crisis grows, Bahr seizes more and more power, and the unpleasant side of his personality becomes more evident. The elaborate plot to rejuvenate American civilization may have inadvertently precipitated something even worse. Ultimately his mistress claims publicly that he is impotent which drives him into a murderous rage and subsequent mental breakdown.

Although this is well enough written, Bahr is such a repulsive character that it is impossible to sympathize with him or his problems. Nor is the society he represents a free one despite the trappings of democracy and the rule of law. There is a good deal of rather silly psychological jargon about spaceships as phallic symbols and caves full of computers as Oedipal substitutes. There are also internal contradictions. At one point we are told that no one is obligated to submit to psychological testing and conditioning unless they hold a government position, but at another point it is mentioned that publishers would be compelled to undergo the treatment if they published any science fiction (A character transparently John W. Campbell Jr. is burned to death by an outraged mob.)

Nourse's final young adult novel was *Raiders from the Rings* (1962). Earth has cut off all contact with its colonies on Mars, the asteroid belt, and elsewhere, and is so fanatic about killing everyone not born on Earth that it strains credulity rather badly. Ben Trefon is a young spacer who is about to participate in a raid on Earth to steal food supplies and young women, both required apparently to keep the colonies functional. His father tries to dissuade him because he believes that something big is underway on Earth and that it bodes no good for the offworlders. The raid is an apparent success, even though as per the formula the young raiders are not armed with lethal weapons.

Ben captures a girl, but ends up with her brother aboard his ship as well, which is a strict violation of the rules. The setup for this one is very poorly thought out. Although the spacers have many agents on Earth, none of them have had any warning that a gigantic space fleet has been constructed. But the two teenagers Ben kidnaps both know about it and it is apparently common knowledge. And if the spacers have the technology to build large fleets of spaceships of their own, why don't they have the ability to create hydroponic gardens so they don't have to raid Earth for food?

The Earth fleet destroys most of the installations on Mars including Ben's home, where his father has apparently died, leaving behind some mysterious artifacts with a note urging Ben to take care of them. As the survivors converge in the asteroid belt in order to counter attack, Ben and his involuntary passengers pursue a devious course to join them, but in the process they find an anomaly on their radar, which is identified as an alien spaceship. The aliens eventually turn out to be benevolent, and in fact Ben's father had secretly communicated with them at some time in the past. The story falls rapidly to pieces from this point onward. The aliens cannot intercede for some reason, although they admit they have done so in the past. And then they intercede anyway. Our hero and his friends convince a spacer woman to sing a song of their history which is so compelling that it leads to a truce. Not only is this unconvincing but the entire sequence in which the humans agree to listen to the song is inconsistent with what we've been told about them previously. This is the weakest of Nourse's young adult books.

The Universe Between (1965) is actually a fixup of two previously published stories. The opening sequence involves a scientific experiment which appears to open a peephole into another dimension. The first several people who look through it die or are driven mad, but then a young woman with unusual adaptive qualities is recruited. She decides not to reveal what she has seen but instead finds a method of crossing into the other realm by a power of will, much to the frustration of all concerned.

The story then jumps forward to the year 2001, in which there is a world government and universal peace, but with almost all raw materials in short supply. The inner solar system has been explored and there are plenty of resources there, but it's far too expensive to move them across space with rocketships. To this end, the scientist from the opening sequence is running a project to build a working matter transmitter, although once again he is encountering funding problems. On the brink of being shut down, the scientific team achieves what they were aiming for, but impossibly the matter transmission is taking place even though the equipment is only partially assembled. This suggests that some other force is at play. Nourse ignores, or doesn't consider, the fact that matter transmission as he describes it would allow one to resend the same signal repeatedly, thus creating multiple copies of the original and therefore solving all the resource problems instantaneously.

The same day that the scientists have their breakthrough - their enthusiasm muted by the fact that objects don't always reappear exactly as they were to start with - the southern end of Manhattan Island mysteriously disappears. The woman from the earlier experiment is now married and has a teenage son who can also enter and exit the other dimension. The son is adept at moving back and forth to the Other World, which is inhabited by inexplicable intelligent creatures who have, until now, ignored his presence in their plane of existence. The matter transmission experiments are disrupting their universe so they continue to snuff out parts of our world as a warning while trying to communicate with the young boy, whom they want to use as a mediator. Eventually he is able to communicate and negotiate a settlement by which cargo can be shifted through the other dimension back to Earth without use of the matter transmitter, so everyone is happy.

Appended to the main story is another set some years afterwards. Humans have now visited the stars and established colonies on Mars and elsewhere. A problem with a shipment from Mars leads to the discovery of a criminal conspiracy and other problems. Both stories are reasonably well told despite considerable oversimplification of the issues and occasional use of deus ex machina solutions to problems. It's also something of a bridge between the author's adult and young adult novels given the aging of the chief protagonist. Some of the speculation about the Other World is interesting but since we know that it is basically impossible for humans to conceive of it, that setting never quite congeals.

There was a substantial gap before Nourse's next novel, *The Bladerunner* (1974). It loaned its name but not its content to the movie version of Philip K. Dick's *Do Androids Dream of Electric Sheep?* Bladerunners are people who acquire illicit medical supplies for renegade doctors who refuse to confine their practice to the government health service in a future dystopia. Given the paranoia about the Affordable Care Act, it's surprising that this hasn't been reprinted to play into those fears. There is also a significant group of people who are opposed to health care of any sort, analogous to those blockading abortion clinics today.

Billy Gimp is a bladerunner who discovers that his room is being bugged by the government, part of a recent pattern of greater intrusiveness. During one clandestine medical visit, the police arrive and arrest Billy, although his doctor partner escapes. Billy realizes quickly that there is something odd about the arrest; there was no effort to capture the doctor and the police seem much more interested in Billy. He is sentenced to surveillance by means of a transponder fastened to his wrist this effectively puts him out of work indefinitely.

While all of this is transpiring, we also learn that a new strain of meningitis, often fatal, is affecting people in the city and the hospital records on the subject are suddenly inaccessible. The doctor has another problem. Hospitals have been using neurological links to surgeons so that robots can be trained to perform complex surgery, a procedure which he opposes because of the lack of human adaptability. To this end he has been sabotaging some of these recordings and the head of the hospital suspects that these "accidents" and "miscues" were deliberate. Eventually we learn that there is a new plague brewing, and that the government has secretly been ignoring the underground medical treatments because it was the only way under the law to get treatment to those not qualified for government care. The plague, however, brings everything out into the open and we are told that the laws will be revisited.

I wasn't entirely convinced that the rising cost of healthcare would lead to large segments of the society rejecting medical care as immoral, but Nourse did foresee that it would inevitably lead to social as well as financial tension. On the other hand, this was a much more restrained, thoughtful, and deliberate novel than any of the earlier ones, though at times the narration slips into lecture mode. The doctor's objection to participating in the program to create robotic surgeons is never really justified - given the shortage of doctors this seems like a good thing. Dystopian novels usually have a government representative as chief villain, but in this case both establishment figures are actually reasonable, flexible, and have good intentions. In fact, there is no villain at all in the novel except the somewhat nebulous one of a bureaucracy constrained by its own rules. This was the first sign that Nourse might evolve into a serious and notable author of adult science fiction, but unfortunately he only wrote one more genre novel during his career.

The Fourth Horseman (1983) was Nourse's last novel, packaged as a mainstream thriller, although he continued to write nonfiction until his death. A forest ranger notices three dead chipmunks, begins to feel ill, and dies the following day. A handful of people who encountered either the woman alive or after her death fall ill as well and it's soon obvious that some kind of mutated form of the Plague is loose. The CDC is particularly concerned because the disease not only spreads much more quickly than normal but it seems to go directly from one person to another rather than through the usual intermediate stage of rats and fleas. Although this is basically a science fiction novel, it has a definite supernatural element. The apparition of a dirty, evil looking, bare footed boy appears to several people who have been infected. As the contagion spreads, Nourse frequently lapses into long discourses on technical details about the cause of plague and the methods used to detect it. A number of minor characters are introduced, only to die or carry on the infection.

Eventually it sweeps across the world, bringing civilization to its knees, although about ten percent of the population survives to rebuild. It has its moments but the pacing is surprisingly slow for a story about a plague that spreads too quickly to be contained.

There were four collections of Nourse's short fiction published during his lifetime. They were *Tiger by the Tail* (1961), *The Counterfeit Man* (1963), *Psi High and Others* (1967), and *Rx for Tomorrow* (1971). Additionally there were many other stories that were not collected at the time. There have been recent collections drawing from all those sources but none of these are generally available. Although his short fiction all appeared in adult markets, the collections were often marketed for young adults. Many of his stories involve medicine or doctors and many but not all involve some degree of space travel. Nourse did try to get his science right, although he didn't always succeed. He seems to have thought that meteor showers would be a major problem in space travel, for example. Some of his stories seem hastily written. They often include plot elements that contradict each other, or problems that the author ignores because it would impede his plot. That said, he also wrote several very good tales including "Brightside Crossing." Some elements in the stories are very dated. There are references to computers still using tapes and punched cards, spaceships carry printed newspapers from planet to planet, etc., but for the most part they hold up reasonably well.

Tiger by the Tail opens with the title story, a nice tale about an opening into a parallel universe and a tug of war that might destroy one or the other reality. In "Nightmare Brother" a man is subjected to a series of hallucinatory ordeals in order to toughen him for interstellar flight, a dubious premise though done well. "PRoblem" has a public relations man trying to convince the public to tolerate the temporary presence of millions of interdimensional travelers. A cure for the common cold has unpleasant side effects in the quite humorous "The Coffin Cure". In"Brightside Crossing" four men attempt to cross the bright side of Mercury but fail and only one survives. The description of the physical conditions there is superb. "The Native Soil" is a humorous problem story. The mud on Venus is valuable but only if the natives can be taught to harvest it. Earth is invaded by nasty critters in "Love Thy Vimp", but they are defeated when people learn to love them. "Letter of the Law" pits a human con-man against a planet whose population believes telling the truth is a weakness.

The title story in *The Counterfeit Man* bears a close resemblance to "Who Goes There?" by John W. Campbell Jr. A spaceship is returning from Ganymede when the ship's doctor realizes that one of the crewmembers has been replaced by an exact duplicate, a shape changing alien intent upon reaching Earth. It's rather clumsily done and far inferior to the Campbell story. At one point the doctor mentions that two of their crew were killed on Ganymede, but actually only one died there. The second man succumbs aboard ship and it is specifically mentioned that he never left the ship during the landing. The doctor makes a fatal error at the end and Earth is doomed but his lack of even rudimentary quarantine precautions makes the whole thing feel rather silly.

"The Canvas Bag" is a mild fantasy about a man cursed never to have a home. "An Ounce of Cure" is a short satire about over specialization, specifically in the medical profession. "The Dark Door" concerns a man who discovers that some people secretly have the ability to function in four dimensions, and he's on the run because they want to kill him to protect their secret. Or is it all an illusion? He was hired by scientists to analyze statistics about insanity. Could he have found something that drove him insane? The ending is meant to be clever but it's not particularly convincing.

"Meeting of the Board" is a frankly reactionary story about a future when workers command a majority of the stock and management is forced into a subsidiary role as the corporations all go bankrupt. The fact that this doesn't actually happen in the real world may not have been evident to Nourse. Eventually the disgruntled management goes on strike against the workers. "Circus" (aka "The Utter Stranger") is very trivial. A visitor from another dimension can't convince anyone that he isn't human. "My Friend Bobby" is about a telepathic toddler who is ultimately abandoned by his family. Nicely written but the end is disappointing. "The Link" deals with a fugitive population of pacifists who fear an invasion by a spacegoing armada. Once again Nourse fails to think about his premise. If the scout who saw them can cross seven light years in a day or so, why would it take the enemy - who have the same technology - weeks or months to travel the same distance? It's an okay story but rather pedantic.

"Image of the Gods" has another scientific problem. A colony on another star could not keep abreast of current events on Earth by listening to radio broadcasts. It would take years to cross the distance between the two worlds. A small colony undergoes turmoil when a more repressive Earth government demands virtual slave labor. The chief villain is clearly defined when he suggests killing the intelligent native race for their fur. The bad guys are thwarted because the natives worship the colonists, although the ultimate fate of the colony is never revealed. "Expert Touch" is set in the same world as *The Mercy Men*. A doctor manipulates a test subject into undergoing a dangerous psychological test, after which the subject refuses to divulge the results. "Second Sight" has an interesting premise. A young woman is a genuine telepath, but since she doesn't need to hear or see anything else, those senses atrophy.

Psi-High and Others actually consists of three loosely related stories and a brief frame in which we are told that these illustrate the three qualities by which the galactic community will judge the human race. "The Martyr", set in the Mercy Men universe, deals with the battle over control of a process that will extend human lifetimes into centuries. It's a minor variation of the standard assumption of many science fiction stories of that period that if we lived longer, we would lose the drive to accomplish anything. The title story, which contradicts the frame rather badly, involves an alien landing on Earth as the prelude to invasion. The frame told us that all aggressive races were quarantined in their own systems, but the invader's race controls half the galaxy. The plot involves efforts to track down the alien with the assistance of one of the rare human telepaths, who are distrusted and feared by the population at large. "Mirror, Mirror" also contradicts the frame with another alien race proving it is vulnerable by panicking. None of these three are particularly outstanding.

Rx for Tomorrow opens with "Symptomaticus Medicus", the closest Nourse ever got to other worldly fantasy. There is a parallel universe where mental disease is cured through a pact with demons but biological disease is untreatable. One of the local physicians gets sent to our universe where he trades skills. The next two, "Rx" and "Contamination Crew" are in the same setting as *Star Surgeon*. In the first, a primitive culture is convinced to take modern medical treatment only when it is accompanied by meaningless rituals and in the second an apparently indestructible lifeform manages to get aboard a medical ship. "In Sheep's Clothing" is a very minor piece about a woman impregnated by a malevolent alien that can control other people's minds. "A Gift for Numbers" is a mildly humorous story about a bookkeeper around whom extraordinary events occur.

"Free Agent" has an interesting set up but the plot is flawed. Selected individuals can be restored to comparative youth by a medical process, after which they spend one year in which they are above the law while adjusting to their new personalities. Why they would be allowed this latitude is never explained, nor how they are financed during that period. A greater flaw is that the protagonist smells a rat when he cannot trace several other people who have undergone the treatment. This makes no sense because he was told in advance that they would be legally dead and untraceable unless they wanted to be found. It's all part of an elaborate and unconvincing program to have people travel to other stars.

"The Last House Call" envisions a dystopian future when doctors no longer make house calls. We're living in that one already. "Grand Rounds" has a demon coming to Earth to discredit a doctor who has saved too many patients. He fails. "Bramble Bush" is set in the same world as "Psi-High" and deals with difficulties helping children born telepathic. "Heir Apparent" is a retrospective look at a man who helped open up the solar system for colonization, from the point of view of the one who married the girl he left behind. "Plague!" is little more than a vignette about the onset of a terrible plague, but it foreshadows *The Fourth Horseman* in its evocation of a raggedy child as the harbinger of the pestilence.

There were many uncollected stories which can be found in quite a wide variety of now mostly extinct SF magazines. "Journey for the Brave" is about the tension preceding the first moon landing. "The Fifty-Fourth of July" is set after an economic collapse destroys civilization, brought on at least in part by the space program. Conflict arises about the potential destruction of the last functioning rocketship. Nourse used this theme more than once. A young boy wants to run away to space in the very minor "Wanderlust." "A Miracle Too Many", written in collaboration with Philip H. Smith, is a fantasy in which a doctor discovers that he can heal people by touching them, but it's a curse not a blessing. "Hard Bargain" is a minor deal with the devil variation. "The Compleat Consummators" is short but effective. A computer dating service is so good at finding people ideally suited to each other that one couple literally merges into a single personality.

"Marley's Chain" is a gimmick story. The protagonist is shunned by everyone on Earth and it's not until the end that we find out that it's because he's White. "Bear Trap" was labeled a novel by *Fantastic Universe* but it's only a novelette. A prominent Secretary of State dies and a journalist decides to buck the establishment and write a true story about the man's life. Although he was noted as a pacifist, he was actually trying to precipitate a world war so that there would be a technological jump that would lead to space travel. "Consignment" is trivial; an escaped convict hitches a ride on an automated highway and ends up being dumped into a blast furnace. "Q-B-B" is a longish and not very interesting space opera involving the breakdown of interstellar communications. A heckler discovers that a performing magician is using genuine magic in the minor but cute "Magic Show." A man uses an android to fill in for him with his wife in "Prime Difference" only to discover that she has done the same. A man married to a witch gets his comeuppance in "What a Place the World Would Be."

Although Nourse never quite made it into the first rank of science fiction writers, he was reliable and generally entertaining but he will, alas, probably become ever more obscure with the passage of time because he wrote a relatively small body of work among which there are only a few short stories that are truly memorable.

H. BEAM PIPER

H. Beam Piper is remembered primarily for his Fuzzy novels and his alternate history stories. Although respected even during his lifetime, he was neither a prolific nor a commercially successful writer and his career was cut short by his suicide. Readers sometimes confused Piper with H.B. Fyfe, a contemporary, despite their very different writing styles because of the coincidental similarity of their names. Piper started writing in the late 1940s and some of his work appeared posthumously. In addition to his science fiction, he wrote a mystery novel, *Murder in the Gun Room*, which was awkward and sold poorly.

Piper's first published novel was *Uller Uprising* (1952), part of the short lived Twayne triplet series in which three short novels were collected in one hardcover edition. Although a shorter version appeared in *Space Science Fiction* magazine, the full text was largely unavailable until Ace reprinted it in 1983. The novel is about the evils of imperialism and chauvinism. Humans have effectively taken control of the planet Uller, whose inhabitants are partly silicon based hermaphrodites. The local military authorities treat the natives much like you would expect, with patronizing contempt and casual brutality. They are currently engaged in attempting to suppress bands of cannibals, which sounds noble enough but they are only doing it to fulfill contracts with the local nobles.

Unfortunately, a charismatic leader has arisen and there are plots to remove the current king and replace him, but no one is certain about the power hierarchy among the plotters. The Ullerans also have been stealing domestic animals from the human settlement for reasons no one understands. The human contingent has differing opinions about how the locals should be treated. One faction advocates deposing the local rulers and administering things directly, while others insist that the natives should be allowed to maintain their own government and customs, although even here there are disagreements about the degree of autonomy they should be granted. It is all clearly a parallel to the British occupation of India, eventually including the Mutiny.

The manifestations of imperialism are obvious. Humans call the natives "geeks", insist that they are brutal and treacherous by nature, and cannot understand why they aren't immensely happy to be granted the gifts of superior civilization. Piper's treatment is not one sided. He also demonstrates that the outside intervention has been beneficial to most of the natives and that some who have more progressive attitudes are actively interested in developing under the tutoring of the humans.

The plot thickens when one of the locals poisons the human governor and there is a minor plot flaw here because in a military/commercial organization like this there would almost certainly be a clear hierarchy of command. Piper suggests that no one knows who would take charge in the crisis and so a committee attempts to organize things. A general assumes control and the bulk of the book consists of the efforts by the new government to contain the rebellion, move friendly troops into more advantageous positions, and kill as many of the enemy as possible. Toward the end they discover that the secret master of the rebellion probably has at least one working nuclear weapon and the situation appears dire for a while before the humans ultimately prevail.

Ultimately Piper sides with the imperialists despite their faults and justifies the wholesale slaughter of the insurgents, which in fact reflects what happened during the Sepoy Mutiny. Some readers might take umbrage because the female characters are all described as "girls" while the males are "men". On the other hand, Paula Quinton - a civilian whose attitudes change dramatically when the rebellion breaks out - is a strong and competent character. There is an interesting suggestion in Piper's naming of minor characters. Three of the characters are named Retief, O'Leary and Falkenberg - characters created by Keith Laumer and Jerry Pournelle, but since none of these had been created yet, and since both Laumer and Pournelle expressed admiration for Piper, it seems possible that they borrowed them from this source. It also was the first story in a loosely knit future history of the Terran Federation, formed mostly by colonists from the southern hemisphere of Earth after a nuclear war devastated most of the rest of the world.

Crisis in 2140, written in collaboration with John J. McGuire, was originally published in 1953 as *Null ABC*, probably a reference to A.E. van Vogt's Null-A novels. It's a dystopian satire set after the fourth world war wherein society is split among the majority, Illiterates, and a privileged minority, the Literates, who are despised by the other group. The authors make some gestures toward explaining how such a society would work but it is superficial because this is meant to be satire rather than a realistic portrait of a possible future. Much of the nonsense the book pokes fun at is still an issue today - including parental objections to school content that should not be controversial, male chauvinism, violence in schools, too easy access to firearms, and anti-intellectualism.

The plot revolves around an election in which a secret cabal among the Literates is backing the leader of the Illiterates. This is part of a complicated strategy that also involves clandestine reading classes designed to return general literacy to the population. That trend is opposed not only by the Illiterates but by those Literates who enjoy their monopoly of influence. The climax includes a lengthy battle - and a deadly one - among armed factions in the middle of a department store. The story actually ages reasonably well except that satire has gone out of fashion in recent years.

Piper and McGuire collaborated again on *A Planet for Texans* (aka *Lone Star Planet*) in 1958. It is quite short and despite the cover on the Ace paperback there are no giant steers on the planet New Texas, settled by Texans obviously. They are not part of the human federation despite the fact that they are the major producers of meat - a native lifeform something like a hippopotamus. They also live in a Libertarian dream state, an unlikely society where everyone is armed (and wears cowboy boots) and a romanticized version of the Old West is the model for their society.

The protagonist is Stephen Silk, a newly appointed ambassador who is supposed to foil an alien invasion and convince the New Texans to join their alliance, without getting killed in the process, which is what happened to his predecessor. Other ambassadors have gone insane, committed suicide, or turned native. Silk has the uneasy feeling that he is being sent to his death to provide a pretext for an armed takeover to pre-empt a conquest by the aggressive aliens, who are descended from canine ancestors. The novel is satirical - no one could take the setting seriously - and includes ingroup jokes like having one of the minor characters named Wilbur Whately, although there is no Lovecraftian flavor otherwise. Politicians can be killed without legal consequences so long as they deserve it, as determined by the courts, and diplomats are politicians, which makes Silk fair game as well. There is some really noxious stuff along the lines of an armed society is a polite society and it's not clear whether or not the authors saw the absurdity of their own arguments. The last third of the novel is a convoluted trial scene in which Silk outwits the aliens, their human allies, and the idiosyncrasies of local law. Minor but not awful. When Ace reprinted it some years later, all references to McGuire were dropped.

Four Day Planet (1961) is a young adult novel set on Fenris, a barely tenable planetary colony whose "year" only lasts four local days, and it is related vaguely to *Uller Uprising*. Walter Boyd is a teenage reporter for the only newspaper on the planet who at the opening of the story is waiting at the spaceport for the arrival of a prominent travel writer. Except that Walter does a little checking - which doesn't seem to have occurred to anyone else - and can't find any evidence that the man has ever written anything.

The local society is a libertarian wet dream. Everyone, even the minors, carry firearms routinely and what government there is consists mostly of thugs. The union, which governs the planet's export buiness, is being run by a corrupt gang who are taking the profits themselves and silencing anyone who opposes them. Another factor is Bish Ware, a secretive spacer who is generally believed to have been important at some time in the past, before being banished to this backward part of civilized space. Some of the exporters - the product is an analogue of verdigris, a biological product harvested from local sea animals - have decided to negotiate separately with another company, and the fake travel writer is their contact. This sets the stage for conflict between the populace at large and the group of thugs and possibly presages even a planetary civil war.

Our young hero joins a hunting expedition that is crippled by sabotage. There is a fairly lengthy section in which they are stranded that slows the pace of the main plot rather dramatically and to no real purpose. They are rescued and a civil war breaks out, but is temporarily diverted when the bad guys start a potentially disastrous fire. There's a big confrontation at the spaceport and Bish Ware is believed to have sold out to the bad guys until we discover - not surprisingly - that he is an undercover agent for the Terran Federation sent to arrest the head of the gang, which he has now done. Everything is tidied up neatly. Although reasonably well told, there is a problem of pacing and the young adult perspective is occasionally obtrusive.

Little Fuzzy (1962) was the first in a trilogy which has been expanded since by other writers. It remains Piper's most famous book and was a strong contender for the Hugo, although it lost to *The Man in the High Castle* by Philip K. Dick. The planet Zarathustra has only been settled for about fifteen years but it is already the most profitable site for the company that is exploiting it, and they can only exploit it because it has no indigenous intelligent species. Or does it? When prospector Jack Holloway stumbles across the Fuzzies, diminutive creatures who appear to be sentient, that possibility threatens the company's profit margin so a host of authorities are called upon to debunk the story, while others prepare to wipe out the species just for safety's sake. There is some questionable science here. The scientists insist that sapience is either present or not, that there are not degrees of it, but then they say that there is no generally accepted definition of the term. On the other hand, particularly during the trial, the discussion of what constitutes sapience is fascinating.

Tension between the two human camps builds steadily while the Fuzzies, initially at least, are unaware of it. At the same time, the military authorities on an orbital base are monitoring the situation and are considering the possibility of intervening. The plot ticks up a level when one of the company men kills a Fuzzy and his own bodyguard is killed during the subsequent turmoil. Jack is accused of murder but his defense is that he was trying to prevent the murder of a sapient being, which would make the company man the killer, as well as invalidating their charter. The company seizes the Fuzzies as evidence but the court rules against them. Unfortunately, the Fuzzies have managed to escape during the interim. Everything comes to a head during the double murder trial and the company loses its charter. This continues to be a satisfying novel both as pure adventure and as a serious speculation about what it means to be intelligent.

The Cosmic Computer (1963, aka *Junkyard Planet*) is set in another one of those gun toting utopias that only works because the author stacks the cards so that it does, ignoring the contradictions and plain silliness of the society as depicted. The planet Poictesme is a backward planet abandoned by an extensive military establishment during an interstellar war with its population reduced to excavating old military sites and selling the salvage. There have been rumors of a super computer somewhere on the planet and our young hero, Conn Maxwell, was sent to Earth to ferret out its location. Instead he learns that it never really existed - which makes sense because if it had there would be others in the Federation - but he uses the search as an excuse to goad his fellow citizens into building a ship capable of travel among the stars.

Unfortunately the society is so badly portrayed that it is hard to summon any sympathy for the protagonists - who look down on the unemployed as tramps and issue such mindless cliches as "guns don't make trouble; people make trouble." Piper's enthusiasm for weapons - no one on the planet is considered dressed unless he has a sidearm strapped on - found its ultimate form when Piper took his own life with one. Women, of course, are exempt. Duelling to the death is legal. And naturally the "liberals" have destroyed effective government on both Earth and Poictesme. And equaly naturally the protagonists are heroes despite lying to the people who supported them because, as the author has arranged, they turn out to have chosen the right path.

This kind of one dimensional society building and plotting is endemic to science fiction - not just by libertarians like Piper - and it is one of the reasons why so much of it can be and is dismissed as trivial. The supposedly enlightened privileged class proves to be repressive of anyone less fortunate, impressing laborers by declaring them vagrants, and generally referring to the unemployed - through no fault of their own - as hoodlums. Piper endorses all of this as well as summary execution of prisoners later in the story.

Once Piper leaves the politics behind, the story picks up. Conn has managed to discover the location of secret bases on the planet which can now be reopened and exploited. The military equipment comes in handy because the planet is plagued by highly armed gangs of bandits with whom it is hard at times not to feel sympathy given the incompetence of the local government and the general malaise and poor conditions endemic on Poictesme. They defeat a band of pirates and acquire half interest in a ship that could potentially satisfy their requirements. Eventually they have an interplanetary ship with which they visit a massive shipyard, also abandoned, on a lifeless, airless planet. After evading some maintenance robots that consider the intruders a form of trash to be swept up, they explore and reactivate the shipyard.

ARCHITECTS OF TOMORROW

Piper has an ambivalent attitude toward his female characters. On the one hand, a number of them are competent technicians and at least one is an authority figure. On the other hand, the males are all "men" and the females are all "girls". Extremist factions who believe that the super computer is Satan battle with others who think it will usher in a new age begin battling all over Poictesme in a rather unconvincing series of encounters. Much to everyone's surprise - except the reader's - they eventually uncover what appears to be a super secret installation and some references to the project. (Piper overestimates the space needed for a super computer, which is probably the most dated thing in the novel.) They learn eventually that the computer projected the collapse of the Federation, which would be much worse if word got out in advance, so they decide to let the computer determine whether or not it should be destroyed. Contrary to Piper's statement, however, no computer is infallible. Despite the quibbles above, this was quite entertaining if not entirely plausible.

Space Viking (1963) is set after the fall of the Federation. The various worlds are self governing and most have regressed into a kind of medieval costume drama with robots. Our hero is Lucas Trask, son of a prominent family on one such world. Although the politics are less intrusive this time around, Piper expresses disdain for democracy, labor unions, and governments in general, showing a preference for a monarchy, private duels, and an armed society. In fact, Piper tells us, in a situation where the citizenry isn't armed: "If their ballots aren't secured by arms, they're worthless." He even suggests that slavery can have beneficial results in the long run. Trask expresses his lack of concern if the Viking pirates slaughter thousands of innocents on other planets so long as they don't upset his business concerns. Trask's bride is murdered on their wedding night by a deranged nobleman who steals a ship and escapes, so he undergoes an immediate conversion and decides to become a Viking himself and search the galaxy for the killer. Trask is conflicted about the damage he inflicts once he has a base and begins attacking helpless settlements, but that doesn't stop him from shooting defenseless people without a word of warning. To be fair, he is repelled by what he has become, but that doesn't stop him from doing it again.

ARCHITECTS OF TOMORROW

Most of the novel consists of Trask's efforts to build a stable base on the planet Tanith, deal with the corrupt king who has assumed the throne back on his home world, set up a viable interplanetary trade organization, and recruit ships to be his allies in the inevitable confrontation with his old enemy. Years pass in fact with very progress on the latter front, although Trask is arguably now more powerful and certainly more popular than the king to whom he is theoretically subordinate. The story moves well until Piper feels called upon to inveigh against government once more and we are subjected to a lecture about how governments should not do anything "for" people and that the best way to have the leaders bow to public opinion is by assassinating them when they don't. The parallel with, say, the Russian revolution does not seem to have occurred to him.

One of the fatal flaws in the novel is that in his quest for vengeance, Trask proves himself to be no better than his enemy, capable of slaughtering innocent people either by mass bombings or at close hand - at one point he kills an unarmed civilian he finds crying over the body of his wife. Another is that Piper does not seem to understand his own contradictions. While praising societies where popular uprisings eliminate unresponsive leaders, he presents the revolutionary movement on one planet - which is doing just what he said societies should do - as an evil scourge that threatens civilization. The great evil they propose, incidentally, is clearly our own social security pensions. Characters whom Piper likes "argue" while those he creates as straw men "rant" or "shriek." Piper envisions an "enlightened" ruling class that doesn't abuse its privileges, supervising the masses, who are simply constrained barbarians. Leaving aside the politics in their own right, the constant lecturing in the last third of the novel destroys its momentum and by the end, most readers are unlikely to care which of the villains actually wins.

The Other Human Race (1964) was the second Fuzzy novel. Recognition that Fuzzies are intelligent beings causes as many or more problems than it solves. The aftermath of the revocation of the Zarathrustra Company's charter has left a power vacuum and political chaos on the planet. Piper demonstrates considerably more political sophistication in this one than in some of his earlier work. Although the company is in one sense the bad guy, it becomes apparent that they share common interests with the new colonial government and that both would be better served by working cooperatively against the criminal elements inevitable within the population. The head of the on planet group, who was chief villain in the first book, becomes a major protagonist this time. He has decided to accept the inevitable and acquires a Fuzzy companion of his own, to whom he grows attached. This complete reversal is a bit of a stretch but Piper brings it off pretty well, and it would certainly be completely credible if this was a standalone novel. Although very little actually happens in the novel - which deals with the various problems that arise now that Fuzzies have been recognized as sapient - it is surprisingly engrossing. Piper's storytelling skills were considerable. Eventually the primary problem is that the Fuzzies have a biological condition that will lead to their eventual extinction and there appears to be no way to reverse it.

Lord Kalvan of Otherwhen (1965) is actually a fix up of the stories "Down Styphon" and "Gunpowder God." The premise is that there are alternate worlds with varying degrees and kinds of human civilization. One timeline has developed the ability to travel among these worlds and has established the Paratime Police to prevent people from exploiting the other realities other than in the more inconspicuous ways preferred by the authorities. Calvin Morrison is a policeman in our world, one of those realities, who is inadvertently transported from one timeline to another. He walks into the middle of a battle between two lords in a feudal version of North America and his heroics gain him the respect of the people of Hostigos, who are menaced by the aggressive plans of one of their neighbors. He devises a cover story that he was exiled from the far future, although in fact he believes that he has been moved through time to a post-apocalyptic world where civilization is slowly rebuilding and has forgotten its past. What follows is a kind of reversal of *A Connecticut Yankee in King Arthur's Court*.

The manufacture of gunpowder is controlled by the priests of Styphon, but Kalvan knows the secret and sets out to make big enough quantities to give Hostigos a chance against its enemies. He also introduces a few other innovations that the locals can implement quickly, as a result of which he becomes the commander of the army and is betrothed to the local princess. Meanwhile, the Paratime Police have sent an agent whose mission is to kill Kalvan before he disrupts things too much, although it is probably too late by the time he arrives and in due course he decides to let things develop as they will. After defeating a variety of enemies, Kalvan is proclaimed High King. Most of the book consists of battle sequences but Piper is one of the few writers of military SF who can make these things inherently interesting.

The third Fuzzy novel, *Fuzzies and Other People*, was not published until 1984 because the manuscript was lost for a long time following Piper's death. It starts only months after events in the previous book. The human government is still working out the various problems caused by the discovery that the Fuzzies are intelligent, and the Fuzzies are being taught to speak so that humans can understand them. This is the first time in the series that we see part of the story from a Fuzzy viewpoint - primarily a group who are not initially aware of the existence of humans. There is a moderately interesting legal case about whether or not the Fuzzies, who are legally children, should actually be considered adults in the courts.

The villainous lawyer from the previous book is back defending a pair of humans who used Fuzzies to commit a robbery. It lacks, however, the intensity of the legal battle in the first book and in fact this is by far the weakest in the series. There is also a planet wide election thrown into the mix and additional problems because Fuzzies can't testify since their statements cannot be verified by a kind of super lie detector used in all legal cases. Then the original Little Fuzzy goes missing. Despite the myriad subplots this time around, there is little tension and not much more momentum. It is possible that Piper planned another draft before submitting it, but it's not clear that he could have done much to remedy its problems.

Paratime (1981) brings together the remaining four Paratime Police stories, plus an unrelated one about alternate worlds. "He Walked Around the Horses" is based on the actual disappearance of a British diplomat in 1809 and speculates that he may have stepped into an alternate reality. "Police Operation" was the first Paratime story and it includes a lengthy lecture about how the various realities came to exist, which is mostly doubletalk and irrelevant to the plot, which involves the search for an alien predator inadvertently let loose in what appears to be our timeline by a now dead traveler who broke the rules. Piper really hadn't found his way with the series yet and the story stumbles rather than races to a conclusion.

"Last Enemy" is set in an alternative timeline where it is possible to communicate with the spirits of the dead and where reincarnation is routine, which I always felt rather contradicted the premise of the series despite other references to personality surviving the death of the body. There is a woman to be rescued there, along with a host of assassins and the prospect of a civil war. Good in parts but Piper throws in too many different elements together here to get a consistent mix. "Time Crime" is novella length. Someone has kidnapped scores of people from one timeline and sold them as slaves in another, which is very much against the rules. Although not as good as the two parts of Lord Kalvan, the story is quite satisfying, involving a massive illegal operation and the Paratime Police's efforts to uproot it and reverse the damage that has resulted. The final story is "Temple Trouble", which looks in more detail at how inter-timeline commerce works. It's short and pretty minor.

Empire (1981) collects four longish stories set within a consistent future. "The Edge of the Knife" is a very good story about precognition in which a history professor gets into trouble when he inadvertently reveals information he has learned about the future. It falters toward the end, however, because of Piper's gross misunderstanding of how psychiatrists might diagnose insanity. "A Slave Is a Slave" is another thinly disguised political lecture that opens with the forced annexation of a planet into the burgeoning Terran Empire. Piper shows his disdain for democracies right at the outset and quite explicitly, and asserts that the use of force should not be a last resort but a worthwhile option to save time. Much of the story deals with the difficulties of abolishing massive slavery by fiat in a short period of time, and that is handled quite well, if a bit simplistically. Unfortunately the story ends with an extended defense of slavery and autocracy. The lower classes are "just incompetent" and not good enough at administration to rule. "Ministry of Disturbance" is set a considerable time later when the new empire is becoming decadent. It is mostly about palace politics and only moderately interesting. "The Return", written with John J. McGuire, is not really in the same future history. It's a standard post-apocalypse story with a cute but minor twist, the sacred text turns out to be a collection of Sherlock Holmes stories. Last in the book is "The Keeper", also set on a ruined Earth. An old man laments the fall of civilization - apparently due to a new ice age and the evacuation of most of the population - but finds something to value in the wilderness.

Federation (1981) gathers five stories from earlier in Piper's future history. "Omnilingual" takes place during an archaeological expedition and is marred by some minor but irritating chauvinism. There are "girl lieutenants" and "girl ordinance officers" and lots of other "girls" scattered around among the "men." On the other hand, the protagonist is a competent woman. If we accept the assumption that an ancient Martian civilization had sentence structure similar to human languages and published recognizable books and magazines, then this story of a scientist attempting to decipher it is not unconvincing, but that's quite a hurdle to leap. The introduction claims that no one can fault Piper's "anthropology and cryptography" but in fact it's based on a whole series of anthropomorphic assumptions. The first word deciphered, for example, is the Martian word for "month", except there is no reason at all to assume they divided up time that way, or that the glyphs in question refer to a period of time. The protagonist reaches this conclusion because the page on which she encounters it looks like a magazine and the glyph is in the right position for a month. Another scientist concludes that their speaking apparatus was "identical to our own" based on having seen a few statues - no skeletons having been found. The ultimate key to translation is clever though and despite its manifest flaws, this is one of Piper's best stories.

"Naudsonce" is a first contact story in which a contingent of humans attempts to open communications with a primitive race that seems to be stuck in the Bronze Age. It includes the unlikely assertion that human society no longer uses the wheel and that most contemporary humans have never seen one, thanks to the existence of contragravity. They have trouble because the inhabitants of the planet don't interpret sound the same way humans do. This is another of Piper's better stories. "Oomphel in the Sky" unfortunately lapses back into political lecturing. A subject planet ruled by a paper tiger Marxist government has fallen on bad times because of its inner contradictions and only private enterprise has any hope of saving the situation. "Graveyard of Dreams" is a short, slightly different version of *The Cosmic Computer*. The final story in the collection is "When in the Course..." It is apparently an unpublished early version of "Gunpowder God" set on another planet instead of another timeline.

First Cycle (1982) was unfinished at the time of Piper's death and was expanded and completed by Michael Kurland. Characters come and go swiftly in this one. Twin planets give rise to two different intelligent races, and it is their history that is the focus of the book. We follow them through various stages of civilization, the discovery of space travel, first contact with each other, growing tensions, and ultimately their mutual destruction in an interplanetary nuclear war. The depressing conclusion is muted by the fact that we never got to know any of the characters along the way.

All of the remaining short fiction is collected in *The Worlds of H. Beam Piper* (1983). "Time and Time Again" was Piper's first published story. A dying soldier in World War III finds himself back in his own body as a child but with adult memories. "The Mercenaries" posits a group of scientists who have essentially become extra-national and neutral, but who discover that one of their number is a traitor to the organization. "Dearest" is the story of an elderly man who hears another voice inside his head. It's the closest Piper ever came to a story of the supernatural. "Hunter Patrol", written with John J. McGuire, is another time travel story, this time to a future when Earth is ruled by a single man. "Flight from Tomorrow" is a post nuclear war story in which humanity must adapt to living in a radiated world. "Operation RSVP" is a minor epistolary piece about nuclear brinkmanship. "Genesis" involves efforts to colonize primitive Earth by Martians. Survivors of a nuclear war solve a problem in Argentina, one of the remaining habitable parts of the world in "The Answer." "Crossroads of Destiny" is a cute story about parallel worlds and "Day of the Moron" is a minor cautionary tale about putting unqualified people in positions of responsibility.

There has been speculation that Piper might have become one of the major figures in science fiction is he had not taken his own life. He certainly had the storytelling skills to do so, although for some reason his shorter fiction generally lacks the narrative tension of the novels. His tendency to lecture limited his appeal and his polemics often disrupted the momentum of his fiction, but when he had those things under control his stories move with great efficiency. He had a rare ability to make even relatively mundane scenes seem interesting. On the other hand, he might have evolved away from the need to pontificate and become more like Poul Anderson, who could state his case without making the reader feel like an audience. Unfortunately, we'll never know.

ARCHITECTS OF TOMORROW

INDEX OF TITLES

"Academy, The" (88)
"Accept No Substitutes" (96)
"Accountant, The" (86)
Afrit Affair, The (27)
"Agamemnon's Run" (94)
"Aide Memoir" (12)
Alien Harvest (81)
Alien Minds (41)
"All the Things You Are" (87)
"Alone at Last" (90)
"Altar, The" (85)
Alternative Detective, The (85)
And Now They Wake (28)
"Answer, The" (155)
Ascendancies (63)
"Ask a Foolish Question" (87)
"Aspects of Langranak" (91)
Assignment in Nowhere (25)
"At the Conference of the Birds" (93)
"Aurochs Came Walking" (122)
Axe and Dragon (18)
Back of Town Blues
Back to the Time Trap (41)
"Bad Medicine" (87)
"Ballots and Bandits" (33)
"Battle, The" (87)
Beachhead Planet (122)
"Bear Trap" (142)
Bees of Death, The (102)
"Be It Ever Thus" (123)
Bell from Infinity, The (120)
"Beside Still Waters" (86)
Best of Keith Laumer, The (37)
Beyond the Rings of Saturn (103)
Big Show, The (35)
"Big Show, The" (35)
Bill, the Galactic Hero on the Planet of Bottled Brains (79)

"Birthday Party" (38)
Bladerunner, The (136)
Blue Atom, The (107)
"Body, The" (87)
"Body Builders, The" (26)
Bolo (37)
"Bramble Bush" (141)
"Brass God, The" (15)
Breaking Earth, The (19)
"Brightside Crossing" (138)
Bring Me the Head of Prince Charming (79)
Calibre .50 (81)
Call To Arms, A (81)
"Canvas Bag, The" (139)
Can You Feel Anything When I Do This? (91)
"Carrier" (95)
"Castle of Light, The" (16)
Catastrophe Planet (19)
"Challenge, The" (108)
Chaos Fighters, The (104)
"Choice, The" (42)
Chrestomathy (38)
Chronocules, The (55)
"Circus" (139)
Citizen in Space (86)
"City of the Dead, The" (94)
"Clear As Mud" (28)
"Cocoon" (23)
"Coffin Cure, The" (138)
Collected Short Fiction of Robert Sheckley, The (92)
"Combat Unit" (22)
"Compleat Consummators, The" (142)
Complete Bolo, The (42)
"Conquerors' Planet" (95)
Conquest of the Space Sea (103)
"Consignment" (142)
"Contamination Crew" (140)
Continuous Katherine Mortenhoe, The (59)
"Cordle to Onion to Carrot" (90)

Cosmic Computer, The (147)
"Cost of Living" (85)
Counterfeit Man, The (139)
"Counterfeit Man, The" (139)
"Courier" (16)
Crisis in 2140 (144)
Crompton Divided (77)
"Crossroads of Destiny" (155)
"Cruel Equations, The" (91)
"Cultural Exchange" (12)
"Dam Nuisance" (28)
"Danger Is My Destiny" (124)
Dangerous Magic, A (70)
"Dark Door, The" (139)
Darkness Before Tomorrow, The (111)
"Dawn Invader" (89)
"Day Before Forever, The" (23)
Day Before Forever and Thunderhead, The (23)
"Day of the Moron" (155)
"Day the Aliens Came, The" (94)
Day They H-Bombed Los Angeles, The (109)
Deadfall (31)
"Deadhead" (88)
Dead Run (82)
"Dearest" (155)
"Deaths of Ben Baxter, The" (88)
"Deep Blue Sleep" (94)
"Demons, The" (86)
"Destruction of Atlantis, The" (93)
"Devil You Don't, The" (35)
"Dial a Death" (93)
"Diamond Images, The" (124)
Dimension of Miracles (76)
Dimensions of Sheckley (93)
"Dinochrome" (22)
Dinosaur Beach (32)
"Diplomat-at-Arms" (42)
"Diplomatic Immunity" (91)
"Disposal Service" (87)

"Divine Intervention" (93)
"Doctor Zombie and His Little Furry Friends" (91)
Doomsday Eve (106)
"Doorstep" (23)
"Down Styphon" (151)
"Down the Digestive Tract" (91)
Draconian New York (85)
Dramocles (78)
"Dream of Misunderstanding, The" (94)
"Dreamworld" (91)
Drowned Queen, The (27)
"Dukakis and the Aliens" (94)
"Early Model" (87)
"Earth, Air, Fire, and Water" (88)
Earthblood (17)
"Edge of the Knife, The" (153)
Electric Crocodile, The (53)
Embassy (15)
"Emissary from a Green and Yellow World" (94)
Empire (153)
End As a Hero (39)
"End As a Hero" (22)
"End City" (92)
Enemies from Beyond (24)
Envoy to New Worlds (12)
"Expert Touch" (140)
"Eye of Reality, The" (93)
Farce to Be Reckoned With, A (80)
Farewell, Earth's Bliss (49)
Fat Chance (31)
"Fear in the Night" (87)
Federation (154)
"Feeding Time" (89)
"Field Test" (37)
"Fifty-Fourth of July, The" (141)
"Final Examination" (94)
"Final Frontier, The" (108)
"Find Me in Eternity" (124)
First Cycle (155)

"Fishing Season" (90)
"Five Minutes Early" (93)
"Flight from Tomorrow" (155)
Flight from Yesterday (114)
"Fool's Mate" (90)
"Forbidden City, The" (28)
"Forest in the Sky, The" (28)
"Forever" (90)
Four Day Planet (146)
Fourth Horseman, The (137)
"Free Agent" (141)
Future Imperfect (42)
"Future Lost" (93)
Fuzzies and Other People (152)
Galactic Dipiomat (15)
Galactic Odyssey (24)
Galaxy Builder, The (38)
"Gambler's World" (13)
"Game: First Schematic" (91)
Game of X, The (84)
"Garbage Invasion, The" (36)
"Genesis" (155)
"Ghost V" (91)
"Giant Killer" (28)
"Gift for Numbers, A" (141)
"Girls and Nugent Miller, The" (89)
Glory Game, The (35)
Godshome (81)
Gold Bomb, The (27)
"Goobereality" (26)
"Goodbye Forever to Mr. Pain" (93)
"Governor of Glave, The" (16)
"Grand Rounds" (141)
"Graveyard of Dreams" (154)
"Gray Flannel Armor" (88)
Great Time Machine Hoax, The (14)
Greylorn (26)
"Greylorn" (26)
"Grime and Punishment" (28)

"Gunpowder God" (151)
"Gun Without a Bang, The" (88)
"Half Men, The" (41)
"Hands Off" (86)
"Hard Bargain" (142)
"Heir Apparent" (141)
"Helping Hand, The" (93)
"He Walked Around the Horses" (152)
Hoax in Time, A (14)
"Holdout" (89)
"Homeward Bound" (109)
"Hoob Melon Crisis, The" (36)
Hot Wireless Sets, Aspirin Tablets, the Sandpaper Sides of Used Matches, and Something That Might Have Been Castor Oil (55)
Hounds of Hell, The (13)
"Hour of Battle" (95)
House in November, The (29)
"Human Man's Burden" (87)
"Humours, The" (88)
"Hungry, The" (95)
"Hunter Patrol" (155)
Hunter/Victim (78)
"Hunting Problem" (86)
Huntress of Akkan, The (102)
"Hybrid" (21)
If at Faust You Don't Succeed (79)
"If the Red Slayer" (88)
"Image of the Gods" (140)
Immortality Delivered (72)
Immortality, Inc. (72)
"Impacted Man, The" (85)
"In a Land of Clear Colors" (96)
"In a Street of Dreams" (96)
Infinite Cage, The (34)
"In Sheep's Clothing" (141)
"Internal Affairs" (33)
In the House of Dark Music (69)
"In the Queue" (35)
Invaders, The (21)

Invaders Are Coming, The (133)
"I See a Man Sitting in a Chair and the Chair Is Biting His Leg" (92)
"Is That What People Do?" (92)
"It Could Be Anything" (23)
It's a Mad, Mad, Mad Galaxy (26)
"Join Now" (88)
Jongor Fights Back! (99)
Jongor of Lost Land (97)
Journey Beyond Tomorrow (74)
"Journey for the Brave" (141)
Journey of Joenes, The (74)
Judson's Eden (41)
Junkyard Planet (147)
Justice City (68)
"Keeper, The" (154)
"King of the City, The" (27)
King of the Fourth Planet (113)
"King's Wishes, The" (86)
Knight of Delusions (42)
Laertian Gamble, The (80)
"Language of Love, The" (89)
"Last Command, The" (37)
"Last Days of (Parallel?) Earth, The" (93)
"Last Enemy" (153)
"Last House Call, The" (141)
"Last Weapon, The" (90)
"Lawgiver" (37)
"Laxian Key, The" (90)
"Leech, The" (89)
"Letter of the Law" (139)
"Lifeboat Mutiny, The" (88)
"Life of Anyone, The" (93)
"Like Alarm Bells Ringing" (109)
"Link,The" (139)
Little Fuzzy (147)
Live Gold (82)
Lone Star Planet (145)
"Long Remembered Thunder, The" (23)
Long Twilight, The (28)

Long Twilight and Other Stories, The (41)
Lord Kalvan of Otherwhen (151)
"Lost Warship, The" (123)
"Love Song from the Stars" (93)
"Love Thy Vimp" (139)
"Luckiest Man in the World, The" (86)
Lunar Eye, The (116)
"Machine, The" (96)
"Magic, Maples, and Maryanne" (94)
"Magic Show" (142)
"Man from Space, The" (125)
Man in the Water, The (84)
Man Obsessed, A (128)
"Marley's Chain" (142)
"Martyr, The" (Sheckley) (96)
"Martyr, The" (Nourse) (140)
Masque of Manana, The (93)
"Meanwhile Back at the Bromide" (92)
"Mechanical Advantage" (33)
"Meeting of the Board" (139)
"Meeting of the Minds" (89)
"Mercenaries, The" (155)
Mercy Men, The (128)
"Mcssage from Hell" (93)
"Message to an Alien" (35)
"Metal Martyr, The" (124)
Meteor Men (21)
"Milk Run" (88)
"Mind Out of Time" (35)
"Mind Slaves of Manituri" (93)
Mindswap (75)
"Minimum Man, The" (88)
"Ministry of Disturbance" (153)
"Minority Group" (95)
Minotaur Maze (79)
"Miracle Too Many, A" (141)
"Mirror Games" (94)
"Mirror, Mirror" (140)
Missionaries, The (56)

"Miss Mouse and the Fourth Dimension" (93)
"Mnemone, The" (91)
"Mob, The" (95)
Monitors, The (19)
"Monsters, The" (85)
"Morning After" (89)
"Mountain Without a Name, The" (86)
"My Friend Bobby" (139)
"Native Intelligence" (16)
"Native Problem, The"(89)
"Native Soil, The" (138)
"Naudsonce" (154)
"Necessary Thing, The" (90)
"Negotiators, The" (36)
"Never Ending Western Movie, The" (92)
"New Horla, The" (94)
"Nightmare Brother" (138)
Night of Delusions (34)
"Night of the Trolls, The" (26)
Nine by Laumer (21)
Nomansland (67)
"No Ship Boots in Fairyland" (38)
"Notes on Perception of Imaginary Differences" (91)
Notions Unlimited (88)
Now Comes Tomorrow (122)
Null ABC (144)
Odyssey (42)
"Odor of Thought, The" (90)
"Of Death What Dreams" (41)
"Off Limits Planet" (95)
Omega (73)
"Omnilingual" (154)
Once There Was a Giant (38)
"On Pain of Death" (122)
"Oomphel in the Sky" (154)
"Operating Instructions" (95)
"Operation RSVP" (155)
Options (77)
Other Human Race, The (150)

Other Side of Time, The (17)
"Other Sky, The" (27)
"Once of Cure, An" (139)
"Palace Revolution" (13)
"Pandora's Box – Open With Care" (93)
"Paradise II" (89)
Paratime (152)
"Pas de Tros of the Chef,, the Waiter, and the Customer" (91)
People Trap, The (90)
"People Trap, The" (90)
"Perfect Woman, The" (94)
Perfect Woman and Other Stories, The (94)
"Petrified World, The" (91)
"Piecemakers, The" (33)
Pilgrimage to Earth (87)
"Pilgrimage to Earth"
"Pime Doesn't Cray" (33)
"Placement Test" (22)
"Plague!" (141)
"Plague, The" (35)
"Plague Circuit" (91)
Plague of Demons, A (13)
Plague of Demons and Other Stories, A (41)
Planet for Texans, A (145)
"Planet of the Gods" (100)
Planet Run (20)
"Planet Wreckers, The" (26)
"Police Operation" (152)
"Policy" (12)
"Potential" (89)
"Prime Difference" (142)
"Prince and the Pirate, The" (16)
"Prize of Peril, The" (88)
"PRoblem" (138)
"Proof of the Pudding" (90)
"Propitiation of Brullamagoo, The" (41)
"Prospector's Special"
"Protection" (87)
"Protest Note" (16)

"Protocol" (12)
"Psi-High" (140)
Psi-High and Others (140)
"Q-B-B" (142)
Quality of Mercy, The (43)
"Quijote Robot, The" (94)
Ragnarok (65)
Raiders from the Rings (134)
"Rank Injustice" (42)
"Redfern's Labyrinth" (90)
"Refuge for Tonight" (108)
"Relic of War, A" (35)
"Restricted Area" (90)
Retief! (42)
Retief: Ambassador to Space (28)
Retief and the Pangalactic Pageant of Pulchritude (39)
Retief and the Rascals (41)
Retief and the Warlords (25)
Retief at Large (42)
Retief: Diplomat at Arms (41)
Retief: Emissary to the Stars (36)
"Retief: God Speaker" (16)
Retief in the Ruins (40)
"Retief: Long Awaited Master" (33)
"Retief of Red Tape Mountain" (12)
Retief of the CDT (33)
Retief's Ransom (33)
Retief's War (16)
Retief to the Rescue (38)
Retief Unbound (42)
"Retief: War Criminal" (28)
"Return, The" (153)
Return of Jongor, The (98)
Return of Retief, The (38)
"Reverse English" (41)
Reward for Retief (39)
"Right to Resist, The" (42)
"Right to Revolt, The" (42)
"Ritual" (86)

"Robotvendor Rex" (93)
Robot Who Looked Like Me, The (92)
"Robot Who Looked Like Me, The" (92)
Rocket to Limbo (129)
Rogue Bolo (39)
"Rx" (140)
Rx for Tomorrow (140)
"Saline Solution" (15)
"Same to You Doubled, The" (91)
"Sarkanger" (93)
Scavengers in Space (130)
Scudder's Game (64)
"Sealed Orders" (12)
Second Atlantis, The (117)
"Second Sight" (140)
"Secret, The" (41)
Seeds of Gonyl (29)
"Seventh Victim, The" (86)
Seven Tickets to Hell (123)
"Shaggy Average American Man Story, The" (93)
"Shall We Have a Little Talk?" (90)
"Shape" (85)
Shape Changer, The (33)
Shards of Space (89)
"Shootout in the Toyshop" (93)
"Sightseeing 2179" (94)
Sign of the Tiger (133)
Silent Multitude, The (46)
"Silversmith Wishes" (92)
Sinister Paradise (123)
"Sinister Paradise" (123)
"Skag Castle, The" (96)
"Skulking Permit" (87)
"Slave Is a Slave, A" (153)
"Slaves of Time" (92)
"Slow Season, The" (90)
"Sneak Previews" (92)
Soma Blues (85)
"Something for Nothing" (86)

"Soul Buyer, The" (42)
"Soul Makers, The" (124)
"Sound of Bugles, The" (122)
Spaceman (24)
"Spacemen in the Dark" (95)
Space Viking (149)
"Special Exhibit" (90)
"Specialist" (86)
"Squirrel Cage" (95)
Star Colony (37)
"Star-Sent Knaves, The" (26)
Stars Must Wait, The (40)
"Starting from Scratch" (91)
Star Surgeon (132)
Star Treasure, The (32)
Star Wasps, The (114)
Status Civilization, The (73)
Steel Crocodile, The (53)
Store of Infinity (88)
"Store of the Worlds, The" (88)
"Stranger in Paradox" (42)
"Street Scene" (42)
"Stubborn Men, The" (108)
"Subsistence Level" (90)
"Supplicant in Space, A" (92)
Survivors from 9000 BC (1000
"Swamp, The" (93)
"Sweeper of Loray, The" (90)
"Symptomaticus Medicus" (140)
Synthajoy (51)
"Tailpipe to Disaster" (91)
"Temple Trouble" (153)
Tenth Victim, The (75)
"Test to Destruction" (35)
"There Is a Tide"
"There Will Be No War After This One" (93)
"Thief in Time, A" (87)
"Thompson's Cat" (123)
"Three Blind Mice" (41)

"Thunderhead" (23)
"Ticket for Tranai, A" (86)
Tiger by the Tail (138)
"Tiger by the Tail" (138)
"Time and Time Again" (155)
Time Bender, The (18)
"Time Check for Control" (95)
"Time Crime" (153)
Time Killers (72)
Time Limit (83)
"Timesweepers, The" (35)
"Time Thieves, The" (26)
Time Tolls for Toro (123)
"Time Tolls for Toro" (123)
Time Tracks (35)
Time Trap (31)
"To the End of Time" (109)
To the End of Time and Other Stories (109)
To Watch by Night (101)
A Trace of Memory (10)
"Trap" (87)
"Trick or Treaty" (28)
"Trick Worth Two of That, A" (93)
"Triplication" (88)
"Tripout" (91)
"Trip to the City, A" (23)
Trouble on Titan (125)
"Troubleshooter, The" (36)
"Truce of Consequences" (28)
Uller Uprising (143)
"Ultimatum" (15)
Ultimax Man, The (37)
Uncanny Tales
Undefeated, The (36)
"Universal Karmic Clearing House, The" (93)
Universe Between, The (135)
Unsleeping Eye, The (59)
Untouched by Human Hands (85)
"Untouched by Human Hand" (86)

Usual Lunacy, A (61)
"Utter Stranger, The" (139)
"Victim from Space, The" (90)
Victim Prime (78)
Vigilante 21st Century (118)
"Voice" (92)
Void Beyond, The (108)
"Void Beyond, The" (108)
Walk Up the Sky (112)
"Walls, The" (22)
"Wanderlust" (141)
"Warm" (86)
"Warrior Race" (94)
"Warrior's Return" (95)
"War With the Yukks, The" (26)
"Watchbird" (89)
"Way Out, The" (125)
"Weapon, The" (108)
"We Are Alone" (94)
"Welcome to the Standard Nightmare" (92)
"What a Man Believes" (94)
"What a Place the World Would Be" (142)
"What Goes Up" (94)
"What Is Life?" (92)
"When in the Course…" (155)
"When the Spoilers Came" (109)
When Two Worlds Meet (121)
"When Two World Meet" (121)
"Where Tall Towers Gleam" (109)
White Death (83)
"Wicker Wonderland" (16)
"Wild Talents Inc." (95)
"Wind Is Rising, A" (89)
Windows (62)
Wonderful Worlds of Robert Sheckley, The (92)
"Woomy, The"
"Worldmaster" (36)
"World of Reluctant Virgins, The" (124)
World of the Masterminds (109)

World Shuffler, The (30)
Worlds of H. Beam Piper, The (155)
Worlds of the Imperium (9)
"Wormworld" (93)
"Writing Class" (94)
"The Yillian Way" (12)
Zanthar at Moon's Madness (121)
Zanthar at the Edge of Never (119)
Zanthar at Trip's End (121)
Zanthar of the Many Worlds (118)
"Zin Left Unguarded, the Jenghic Palace in Flames,, John Westerley Dead" (92)
Zone Yellow (40)

www.ingramcontent.com/pod-product-compliance
Lightning Source LLC
Chambersburg PA
CBHW061651040426
42446CB00010B/1682